跟雅思考官学雅思

Learning the IELTS with IELTS Examiner

雅思 8 分万能作文

The All-purpose Band 8 Academic IELTS Writing Book

主　编　Alannah T. D. Fitzgerald

　　　　张成思

大连理工大学出版社

Dalian University of Technology Press

图书在版编目(CIP)数据

雅思8分万能作文 /(英)费茨杰拉德(Fitzgerald,A),张成思
主编.—大连:大连理工大学出版社,2005.2(2009.8重印)
跟雅思考官学雅思
ISBN 978-7-5611-2750-6

Ⅰ.雅… Ⅱ.①费… ②张… Ⅲ.英语—写作—高等学校
入学考试,国外—自学参考资料 Ⅳ.H315

中国版本图书馆 CIP 数据核字(2004)第 079729 号

出版发行:大连理工大学出版社
　　　　(地址:大连市软件园路 80 号　邮政编码:116023)
印　　刷:大连业发印刷有限公司印刷
幅面尺寸:185mm×230mm
印　　张:10
印刷时间:2009 年 8 月第 13 次印刷
责任编辑:高　颖
责任校对:刘　雯
封面设计:孙宝福

ISBN 978-7-5611-2750-6
定　价:18.80 元

发行电话:0411-84708842
邮购电话:0411-84703636
传　真:0411-84701466
E-mail:dutp@dutp.cn
URL:http://www.dutp.cn

编者的话

凭栏远眺、目及凌峰······

翻开本书,会发现作者给大家更多的会是激励和鼓舞,留给读者更深的是"立即行动,必能成功"的信念。当大家手中拿到这本雅思作文"机警"的时候,大洋彼岸的作者也在与广大考生和中国的英语学习者共勉。

作者更是大家的英文考试战友。从托福、雅思到 GRE 等等,作者经历了各类英语考试的洗礼,更了解中国考生的弱点,也更能体会广大雅思学习者的心境。所以本书的内容更能贴近读者,更准确地说,是贴近雅思学习备考者。张成思在英国曼彻斯特大学经济学院攻读博士期间,受聘于曼彻斯特雅思中心担任特聘雅思培训讲师,与本书的另一作者——雅思考官 Alannah 共事很久,对考官的评分标准、评判点有很深的了解、很强的把握。作者用他的亲身经历,努力为处在雅思考试作文困境中的读者送上及时雨、雪中炭。更有力的一点是,作者在曼彻斯特大学教学期间,接触到英国本土学生的写作,用英语是母语的人们的眼光去审视我们中国考生会犯的错误,把最地道的表达贯穿于本书的始末。

最后,作为不是英语专业出身的作者,照样成功地通过各种国外的英语考试,能拿到中国最高的英语专业八级证书,能在英文单词鬼魅魍魉的经济学学习中游刃有余,能在鬼佬遍地的曼彻斯特(曼彻斯特大家不熟悉,但是一定知道曼联)担任雅思教师,作为年轻有为一代的你,更能搏击长空,攻下雅思作文关!当你许下"让思念从此毁灭,让灾难不再重现,当爱变得如此真切,从此魂消魄散在三界"的诺言的时候,其实你已经开始向自己挑战了。作者送给大家的是:立即行动,一定成功!

Preface

It is with great pleasure that I address my readers in this preface to *The All-purpose Band 8 Academic IELTS Writing Book*. While I have spent several years in English materials development this book has been my first professional encounter with formatting a bilingual resource book in academic writing. It has been a tremendously rewarding experience for me and my colleague, Mr. Chengsi Zhang, who I came to know while I was conducting research in the field of English Language Teaching (ELT) in the UK in 2002/2003. In saying this, however, it is important to note that rewards often result from challenges that are eventually overcome in the writing process. Both Mr. Zhang and I will attest that the making of *The All-purpose Band 8 Academic IELTS Writing Book* has been no easy feat and that many formats for this book were deliberated upon before coming up with the version of the book you now hold before you.

My experience as an IELTS examiner has given me great insight into the nature of the test (both the general and academic modules) and how test candidates are assessed. This book focuses on IELTS examination tasks and strategies for achieving a high band score in academic writing, and this is further exemplified through useful sample answers which I have provided for users of this book to follow.

The IELTS test was developed with real world communication goals in mind. In particular, the academic module has been designed to enable test candidates to obtain higher education degrees and diplomas from English speaking countries such as the UK, Ireland, Canada, Australia and New Zealand. More importantly, IELTS academic writing tasks reflect actual tasks that are commonly encountered in tertiary study programmes where the language of communication is English.

Currently, I am a faculty member at the International Graduate School of English which is located in Seoul, South Korea. You can visit our school's website to find out more about me and the work I am involved in at: http://www.igse.ac.kr/. Through my work at IGSE I have been directly involved in developing an academic English writing curriculum for students who are writing in English at the postgraduate level. This includes the development of written communication skills in English for Academic Purposes (EAP) along with guidance in research writing for meeting Masters Thesis requirements.

I sincerely hope that my combined experience as an IELTS examiner, English language teacher and teacher trainer will shine through the pages of this book to assist you in developing techniques for academic writing in English. Moreover, I wish you great success in every stage of the writing process.

Alannah T. D. Fitzgerald

序

　　首先,本书是考生朋友的雅思写作"机警"。

　　出国留学的梦想已经慢慢深入到许多在校大学生或者是已经工作了又准备在专业上再上一个台阶的学习者的中间。英语是母语的国家自然成了大多数学生的首选。所以越来越多的学生需要通过雅思考试来实现出国留学的梦想。雅思考试中考生觉得很难拿到分数的是作文部分。而作文部分是申请国外大学录取委员会最看重的一项。原因很简单,一个英文写作能力低的学生,很难适应在国外大学的学习生活。

　　为什么要给大家写一本可以保过8分的作文书呢?

　　有三点主要原因:首先最重要的是,**英国雅思评分机构(剑桥考试委员会)自2004年起对写作要求和具体的评分标准有了极大的改变,而这些改变是中国考生并不真正了解的。**广大考生如果继续延用以往的写作技巧或者甚至死记硬背一些并不符合雅思最新作文要求的作文,很难达到理想的分数。本书的最大特点之一就是完全从剑桥考试委员会的最新要求出发,为中国的广大考生提供最具权威的示范文章,并且每篇范文都给出了详细的阐释,让考生和英语学习者真正把握写作高分的实质,在写作方面有个质的提高。

　　其次是考虑为广大英语学习者提供一个正确、权威和有效的雅思写作指导。而最权威的人物就是雅思考官! 本书所有内容都经过了雅思考官 Alannah Fitzgerald 的审核。正文部分的满分示范范文都是 Alannah 的手笔,所以大家可以有机会品味真正的原汁原味的满分文章!

　　写这本书的另外一个原因就是为了填补雅思写作书籍的一些空白和盲点。作者看过很多雅思写作方面的书籍,虽然有的书中给出的"模板"很受欢迎,在应考上却显得有些不奏效。因为光有模式,没有变化的句式和词汇表达,考生很难灵活变通。再有,由于网络的发达,许多考生在网络上看到的所谓"范文"实际上却有许多错误。更严重的情况是给出的文章本身错误很多,而如果基础不是很好的读者,可能会被误导。可以想象一下,在考试中你默写下了一篇这样的文章,怎么能得高分呢? 所以本书的一个很重要的目标就是为广大学习者和备考者提供一本真正的范文背诵书。当然,仅仅机械的死记硬背效果可能还是不会理想,因为雅思作文要求词汇、句式、语法的多变性。本书考虑了这个方面,在各种分析或者是相关的解析中都做了灵活应用的示范和解释,大家只要精心翻看书中的相关内容,就能一目了然!

　　本书的选材、题目等极力贴近雅思真题,也就是真正的考试题目。这并不等于说不做拓展,或者是选材狭窄。恰恰相反,在对选定的各类题目阐释说明的过程中,作者们却花费了大量的精力查询和阅读最新最权威的雅思书籍。国内的许多雅思书是

通过直接引进英文原版的方式。而得益于身处英国的优势,作者们参阅的都是国外最有力度的书目。其中主要包括:

IELTS PLUS(2002),　　　*Cambridge IELTS 1, 2, 3, 4*(*forthcoming*, 2004),

Insight IELTS(2001),　　　*Preparing for IELTS*(2003),

A Book for IELTS(2000),　　*Focus on IELTS*(2003),

IELTS Essay Writing(2004)

　　另外,一本好书的写就,绝不仅仅是作者一己的功劳,这其中要感谢的人很多。首先要感谢的是大连理工大学出版社的遆东敏女士。应该说没有她对本书的策划,没有她一如既往的鼓励,真的不会有这本(套)雅思写作书的问世。她从一开始约稿到整本书的撰写过程中,都不遗余力地给予我和 Alannah 两位作者精神上的鼓励。还有,虽然作者手中的雅思作文素材很多,但要把教学的讲义和手边的素材编辑整理成为一本适合读者阅读的好书,要比我们想象的难多了。还是遆东敏女士专业建议给作者们提供了极大的帮助。

　　这本雅思作文书的出版同时还要感谢同在曼彻斯特雅思中心(Manchester IELTS Centre)教学的美国同事 Joseph 的热情帮助。尤其是书中第二部分的"Writing Task 2 各种问题归类概括"一节,得到了 Joseph 的慷慨帮助。Joseph 对作者的范文提供了修改意见和句法方面使用的建议。

　　另一个要感谢的是上海交通大学英语学院的胡开宝教授。在作者策划写作的过程中,恰逢胡老师在曼彻斯特大学访学。胡老师对学问的一丝不苟的精神对作者有很深的启发。胡老师是大家使用的《大学英语》的主编,对英语教学非常有见地。关于雅思写作,作者在和胡老师的交谈和讨论中受益匪浅。当然更重要的是,在曼彻斯特求学的过程中,胡老师给予的一贯支持和鼓励使笔者深深感动。

　　我还要感谢我的妹妹张新秋,她在文字编辑方面给了我极大的帮助。而也是这种至深的兄妹情谊让我无论在或喜或悲的时候都会很快回到学习和工作中去。作者撰写这本书的时候,她也以优异的成绩通过了日本语国际一级考试。希望这本书的出版也是送给她的一份礼物!她的不倦的奋斗和追求再次鼓舞着我:尽我所能,为正在中国为雅思考试"奋战"的同学们送上一本好的雅思作文书,在你们实现留学梦想的时候,再一起来回想这段难忘的"背书、奋战"时光!

　　本书主编:Alannah T. D. Fitzgerald、张成思;副主编:林英玉、齐丽霞;参加编写的还有:王岩、吴爱丹、安雪花、于桂敏、胡涛、及欣、马建军、黄凤秋。

　　出版是遗憾的事业。编写一本书也不可避免的会有不完美和可能的缺憾,本书如有错误之处,完全是作者的责任,同时希望广大英语学习者给予批评指正。笔不前驰,祝大家在英语学习尤其是雅思备考的过程中披荆斩棘,成功始还!

编　者

2004 年 12 月于英国曼彻斯特

目 录

第一部分

介 绍

Victory won't come to me unless I go to it.

胜利是不会向我走来的,我必须自己走向胜利。

——*M. Moore* 穆尔

1.1 本书导读

　　下面就本册书的内容设计、结构和各部分的关联作系统的说明,这样可以方便不同的读者有目的、有取舍地进行阅读,提高读者的阅读效率。由于中国备考雅思的学生不断增多,所以不同层次、不同背景的使用者可以根据目录和这部分的介绍有重点地阅读本书。对于写作教师,可以根据课程规划和课时安排作摘选。

　　本册写作书由五大部分组成。本部分(第一部分)的第二小节(1.2)简洁地对雅思考试和相关的学习方法作一个综合的介绍说明。而第 3 小节(1.3)综合介绍雅思作文的考试情况。那么很自然的,Writing Task 1(1.3.1 Writing Task 1 综合说明)的相关信息及内容要首先和大家见面。在这部分,综合地就小作文部分作一下说明,并不进入深层的写作技巧内容,因为我们把篇幅留在第二大部分(解读部分)。所说的解读就是要详细到位地让广大读者真正透彻地洞悉雅思作文的要旨! 接下来的小节(1.3.2 Writing Task 2 综合说明),关于 Writing Task 2 部分的综合介绍仍然定位在"短、平、快"的基础上。在这一部分我们主要介绍备考雅思作文以及和雅思写作实际考试要求相关的内容,而详尽、系统的写作思路、写作技能和写作示范的任务放在了下一个大单元(本书的"第二部分")。

　　第二部分通过详尽的讲解说明向广大考生循序渐进地阐释具体的写作思路、套路和写作思维方法。这一部分也是本书的一个小高潮。第一小节集中介绍雅思"Writing Task 1"写作部分的相关内容,也就是我们常说的"小作文"或者叫"图表作文"的内容。图表作文在作文总体评分(9 band)中占 30% ~ 40% 的比重,尽管"小作文"没有"大作文"所占的分数权重大,但是快速有效地完成这一项写作任务,不仅为"大作文"的成功完成留出充足的时间,而且也让我们更有信心地自如应付第二项写作任务,所谓"良好的开端是成功的一半",英文里面我们说是"Well begun is half done."或者"A good beginning almost assures success."说的都是这个道理。这一部分(第二部分)的第二小节覆盖了"Writing Task 2"的写法思路等重要内容。由于这部分的写作内容是考生的难点也是考查的重点,我们具体详尽地分析和示范议论文的写作思路、方法和模式。英文中一篇好的议论文,一定要围绕一个中心思想来行文谋篇,我们给大家的例子示范正是强调这一点。为什么呢? 因为东西方文化的差异,思维模式的不同,自然会需要有一个介入的过程。大家通过了这一瓶颈(bottle neck),往往就会有"柳暗花明"、"豁然开朗"的感觉。实际上,我们在接触到的学生作文中,深切地体会到优秀的雅思作文是相似的,但是糟糕的文章却各有各的毛病,所谓"Good IELTS essays are the same, but poor ones are all different and have their own weaknesses."

有了大致的写作思路之后,我们在第三和第四大部分给大家提供了 15 篇"图表作文"和 30 篇"议论文"的雅思考官范文习作。这部分的范文由雅思考官 Alannah 主笔,主要是希望为大家提供原汁原味的"背诵"范文。我们所强调的并不是"死记硬记",而是讲求灵活的记忆和拓展,将原文中精华的成分融入到每个同学自己的作文中去,也就是所谓的教会大家"捕鱼"的技术,而不仅仅是只给大家提供现成的作文。这个过程体现在对范文中的"万能句子"、"星级词汇"的指点和分析。在每一篇范文后还为大家精选了一小段地道的英文段落,大部分是摘自各类雅思考试参考书中的阅读理解文章,慢慢地大家会对"阅读写作不分家"有更深层的认识。值得一提的是本书提供的大部分雅思写作范文都是作者们在英国"曼彻斯雅思中心"教授雅思课程时使用过的,所以这些文章针对性非常强,主要针对广大考生写作中的弱点,比如说提笔忘词,不知道具体用什么句子内容,或者是拿来一个题目,似乎有许多话要说,却不知道如何开始,似有千言,却是"文头"难开。针对这些问题,主要用"思路"和"观点"(ideas, supporting ideas)来引领读者开辟巧径,以巧制胜,具体内容在本书的第二部分有详尽的阐述。另外,让作者们很欣慰的是我们在撰写雅思范文用作课程培训内容的同时,几乎每一次都会在实际考试中碰到与这些范文同样或者类似的写作题目,也就是所谓的"压题"。但是我们更看重写作思路的提高,这也是本书的最主要宗旨。当然,由于雅思作文问题、目的、内容的局限性(作者经常愿以"雅思出题委员会的成员为了保住这个工作,不至于下岗失业而不得不局限于一定范围出题"来解释这个现象),所以"压题"也只是本书的一个"by-product"。这一部分也可以供教授写作课的英语教师作为写作素材参考。

本书正文的第五部分更是本书的另一个精彩部分。根据以往的经验,每次考试都不会脱离我们所总结及预测的这些题目。这一部分精选了最近、最新、最常考的考题(topics)10 篇,并且对各个题目给出了非常清晰、地道的范文。所有范文都经过反复推敲,和雅思考官共同写成! 品读这里的范文,大家会觉得很容易"下笔有神",因为所给的范文都不是脱离广大中国考生实际情况的。大家只要坚持背诵、改写,所有内容都可以真正成为你自己的东西。这部分内容得益于作者在英国曼彻斯特大学攻读博士学位期间教授雅思课程的经验和经历。每次考试我的学生们都及时地反馈回最新的考试题目和动向,应该说,没有这些经历,也谈不上什么所谓的预测。通过这一部分的学习,大家可以体会到转化题目的技巧,把比较难的题目转化成自己熟悉的有可行性的写作思路的文章。

最后,本书的附录部分是每一个备考雅思的学生一定要吃透的"秘籍"。对于只剩下几周或者是更短时间的应考者,可以投入精力牢牢记住这里为大家汇编的经典雅思写作万能表达法。作者将考官眼中最"抢镜头"的表达分类汇总,作为一个完整的部分放在附录部分,这样大家每时每刻都可以翻到本书的最后部分,抓住任何一刻可以利用的时间,把用来得分的利器背下来。其实雅思高分并不是神话,作者的苦心设计和精心的内容选编,都是为了我们中国考生能够创造高分奇迹,从而缔造雅思考分神话!

1.2　雅思考试综合介绍

4

The great commerce of every civilized society is that carried on between the inhabitants of the town and those of the country. It consists in the exchange of rude for manufactured produce, either immediately, or by the intervention of money, or of some sort of paper which represents money.

Adam Smith, The Wealth of Nations

亚当·斯密在《国富论》中强调货币作为媒介在人类生活中的重要作用。而雅思考试在近年来成为广大中国学生出国留学的不可缺少的媒介和桥梁。如何才能更好更快地适应雅思考试的要求,顺利地通过这门英语语言水平测试呢?

我们中国有句耳熟能详的古语:"知己知彼,百战不殆。"在各类英语考试中,"知彼"更加重要。因为在备考过程中,一定要熟悉这类考试的出题模式、出题套路层次和强调考查的重点,然后才能有的放矢地去准备,更好地弥补自己的不足,在考试中取得理想的成绩。雅思也不例外,在大家准备雅思考试之前,首先要对雅思考试的模式有所把握。由于本书是一本写作书,所以对综合的考试程序和其他三个考试部分(Reading, Listening and Speaking)不做详细的介绍,但是给出作者对其他三个部分的学习建议。留下篇幅对写作部分作深入的阐释,让广大学习者对写作的两篇作文(Task 1 and Task 2)有一个较深的认识和透彻的理解。有一本雅思参考书叫 Insight IELTS,名字非常好,这里借用一下 insight 这个词,形象到位地描述了您手中的这本写作书。希望这本书能成为大家雅思备考的良师益友。

首先,对雅思考试的内容和测试要求我们引用 British Council 给出的说明。IELTS 是 The International English Language Testing System 的缩写。根据 British

Council 官方给出的说明,雅思是所有英语非母语国家的学生进入英国、澳大利亚、新西兰、加拿大以及美国学习所需要通过的语言考试。下面这段话概括了雅思考试的大致内容:

The examination assesses the four essential skills: **listening, reading, writing and speaking.** All candidates receive a Test Report Form (TRF) presenting the scores (on each skill and overall) in terms of BAND SCALES. This indicates the level of your ability in using English. The scores are graded into nine bands from:

BAND 1 - NON-USER: Essentially has no ability to use the language beyond possibly a few isolated words.

to:

BAND 9 - EXPERT USER: Has fully operational command of the language; appropriate, accurate and fluent with complete understanding.

All candidates are tested on listening, reading, writing and speaking. All candidates take the same Listening and Speaking modules. There is a choice of reading and writing modules: academic or general training. ACADEMIC modules assess whether a candidate is ready to study or train in the medium of English at an undergraduate or postgraduate level. GENERAL TRAINING modules are not designed to test the full range of formal language skills required for academic purposes. Instead, they are suitable for candidates who are going to English-speaking countries to complete their secondary education, to undertake work experience or training programmes not at degree level, or for immigration purposes to Australia and New Zealand, Canada and the UK.

正如我们给大家用黑体字显示的内容,雅思和许多英语语言考试测试类似,突出考查听、说、读、写这四大部分。由于本书针对的读者是准备出国留学的考生,而 General Training 是针对工作移民类的考生设计的,所以我们只涉及学术类的写作,也就是我们常说的 A 类(Academic Writing)考试。通常情况,英国等大学的语言成绩要求雅思要达到 6.0 以上,具体情况因各个大学和不同专业有所变化。通常文科类的要求比较高,平均 7.0 左右,工程、理科类的要求稍微低一些。另外一点就是许多人往往有错误的印象,认为申请研究生课程的雅思成绩要比申请本科高。实际上在语言上的要求没有差别。

对"听、说、读、写"的建议和说明:高效地提高口语和听力。

听说是个整体,听是说的基础,说要带动听力的提高。发音标准是听说的前提。把发音学好了以后就会尝到甜头的。这句话是千真万确的,只有能正确读出来才能

5

真正地听懂。让每一个词的发音在大脑里留有一个印象,再一次听到这个词时,就会与大脑里的那个印象相契合并且迅速做出反应,这样就很容易听懂了。

我们建议大家多听、常听收音机英文节目。BBC新闻节目、布莱尔的讲话(英国首相布莱尔的发音和语音语调是极为标准的)、采访等。听力中分为精听和泛听。备考过程中,要精听为主,泛听为辅。有声语言与书面语言不同,往往一闪即逝。因此,在听力训练中,同学们应集中精力,听清、听准。同时,在训练中,要边听边思考,养成良好的听力习惯。

积极有效的办法还有学以致用。在日常的沟通和对话中听。听说结合,互相促进。听懂了,就要模仿着说出来,说给其他同学听。互说互听,互相改正,彼此都有进步,达到口语听力共同进步的目标。

还建议大家有效地结合阅读和写作:

要在规定的时间内(60分钟)高效地完成雅思阅读理解文章,第一个前提就是词汇量。在英国曼彻斯特有一件非常有意思的事情,就是每天在公交车和市中心等人流集中的地方会有人专门负责发放一份由曼彻斯特轻轨(MetroLink)交通公司发行的免费英文报纸(Metro)。和国内流行的一些英文报纸比较起来,最大的差别就是遇到的词汇更丰富多彩了。没事看看,就知道自己的词汇量有多差了。这是一个老生常谈的话题,大家知道,单词是英语的基础,没有单词,就好像建大厦没有砖头,只能是幻想中的空中楼阁。但是背单词又被大家认为是最难、最枯燥的事情。基础好的朋友可以通过阅读学单词,但是对基础不好的,这点根本行不通。整篇文章都看不太明白,还谈什么学单词呢?既然咱们现在水平不行,就要拿出比别人更多的努力。先大背单词30天,然后你一定会发现自己在英文水平上有了一个提高!由于雅思词汇的特点,以及雅思考试所着重考查的"同义转换"(同一个意思,用不同的表达方式或者不同的词汇)的特点,我们建议大家参阅本书的姊妹篇《雅思同义词词汇必备》。

有了词汇量的基础,下一步就是要读、写结合。多看,多读,多模仿。英语开始就要模仿,注意并记住地道的表达方法。一定要有恒心,越是看不明白的东西越要看、要记录。写有用的短语、词句,要把它背下来,熟读熟背。中国的俗语说得好,"熟读唐诗三百首,不会作诗也会吟。"熟读范文,强化记忆一些精彩段落,这是提高雅思阅读和写作能力的必由之路,也是外语语言学习的不二法则。

另外要特别注意"同义转换,变通表达"。在本书的各部分讲解和范文示范中都是句型转换或同近义、反义词转换的阐释,通过这样的练习,使大家思路更加灵活,不至于去走进"死胡同"。"同义转换"这是写作能力提高的"变通器"。而大家熟悉了雅思考试各个部分的内容之后,就会发现实际上听说读写四个部分都非常强调考查考生的这一能力。

提高写作和阅读理解能力的另一个非常有益的训练是缩写课文，或者练习写一篇长文章的摘要（summary），渐离"原文"。这是进一步把握阅读理解、融阅读与写作于一体的强有力的手段，可充分利用刚学过的英语语言，来表达大家要表达的核心内容。

还有一点建议就是掌握一定的写作技巧，如文体、文风、时态和语法以及表达内容的前后呼应，连接用语 in turn, therefore, hence, nonetheless 等恰当、合理的应用。这些语言应用得好，会大大增强文章的说服力、整体感、流畅感和美感。

总之，阅读与写作不分家。阅读和写作能力的共同提高不是一蹴而就的。我们给大家提供的是尽量最优化时间和效率的方法和途径。本书的内容也尽量想考生之所想，解决大家备考的困惑和疑问。只要大家坚持从易到难、从少到多、从范文到实践、从慢到快的循序渐进的原则，激发自己学习英文写作的兴趣和积极性来带动阅读理解能力的提高，加强竞争意识，持之以恒，就一定能成功！Your efforts will pay off and your life will be better off! 想一想写一手漂亮的英文文章的时候，你的生活里也会多一份酣畅淋漓的快乐，为了实现年轻时的追求和梦想，为了将来海外求学的成功，努力吧！

1.3 雅思考试作文部分介绍

The ideal central bank would combine ultimate government responsibility with a high degree of day-to-day independence for the authorities of the bank. It would be desirable to preserve unimpaired authority in the executive officers of the bank, whose duty would be to take a broad and not always commercial view of policy.

John Maynard Keynes

约翰·梅那德·凯恩斯早在几十年前就强调了中央银行独立性的重要。而在雅思写作当中我们强调的却不是"独立性"，而是相关性。更确切一点说，是强调写作和阅读同为一体。实际上，阅读与写作紧密相关，口语与听力密切联系。这里所提到的阅读与写作密不可分，不是简单的从英语学习角度出发，而是在雅思考试中深藏的一条突破途径。阅读与写作都遵循一条核心原则，就是"一心一意"。更具体地说，英文写作的思路比较"死板"，写作一定要按照一个中心思想贯穿到底，不要加入任何与中心无关的内容，更不能为凑字数而随便添加内容。通过在随后的内容里详细的示范讲解大家会有更多的体会。相信经过一段时间的训练，聪明的中国考生一定可以把握写雅思作文的套路层次。

实际上中国学生、考生之所以伟大，就是因为我们有强大的"应付"考试的能力。我们并不把这里的"应付"看作贬义词语，因为我们有切身的体会，在我们把问题分析清楚，把目标(有些同学喜欢称之为"靶子")锁定好了以后，大家就会把握要领，举一反三。而且，雅思8分和满分的成绩都是我们中国考生创造的奇迹！所以我们很有理由相信，在大家读完本册之后，在彻底全面地剖析完雅思作文之后，亲爱的雅思"战友"，会给我们以7分以上的回馈，这也是我们期待的从大家那里得到的最好的回报！

1.3.1　Writing Task 1 综合说明

In order to write about visuals, as required in IELTS Academic Writing Task 1, it is necessary to understand what to write, as well as how to write it.

Gabi Duigu

上面这小段话是一位澳大利亚作者在她的雅思写作书中提及的，实际上给我们一个很好的启示，也就是在写 Writing Task 1 之前，大家要熟悉图表作文中我们要写的是什么，如何去写。关于 Writing Task 1 的详细分类讲解放在本书的第二部分。在这里我们简要介绍一下图表作文考查的考生的能力范围、评分标准等。下面我们用中英文结合的方式给大家说明一下，这样有利于大家更直接地了解和领悟。

The Writing Task 1 tests your ability to fulfill the following functions of English:

• Accurately interpret graphic data and describe main trends and highlight areas of difference therein

• Accurately describe a process or event or sequence of events and explain how something works

The question: You are given graphic or pictorial information and you have to **write a description** of this information.

实际上，在 IELTS HANDBOOK (1999) 上，考试委员会给出了类似的官方说明：

In task 1 candidates(考生) are asked to look at a diagram or table, and to present the information in their own words. Depending on the type of input and the task suggested, candidates are assessed on their ability to:

- Organize, present and possibly compare data
- Describe the stages of a process or procedure
- Describe an object or event or sequence of events
- Explain how something works

经常遇到的内容涉及到：bar charts, line graphs, pie charts and tables often appear in Task 1 of the academic module. However, you could also come across an **object or series of pictures or diagrams or a flow chart** to describe (e.g. "黄石公园火灾后森林的生长情况")。最新的考试经常出现几种图形的综合。但是许多考生对这种题型往往不知道从哪里下手，经常会因此耽误了议论文部分的写作。有鉴于此，本书在后面章节中专门提供了这类题目和写作范文，希望大家仔细研读，多背诵我们提供的范文文章，并加以改装，举一反三，达到短时间内突破图表作文的境界。

If graphs are used there may be just one—usually a line graph or a bar chart. However, there **could also be more than one** of the same type of graph or a combination of graphs and charts. For example, you could get a bar chart and a pie chart together (参阅 Cambridge IELTS 1, p.31) or a line graph and a table.

Writing Task 1 关于写作字数和时间的要求：

You have to write at least 150 words.

You are advised to spend 20 minutes on this task.

图表作文普通评分标准：主要依据以下三点给分。

Task Fulfillment(写作任务的完成情况)

Being able to follow the instructions properly.

Being able to write a clear, accurate and relevant description of the information.

Being able to focus on the important trends presented as graphic information.

Coherence and Cohesion(上下文是否连贯、衔接是否紧密)

Being able to organize your writing using a suitable structure.

Using connective words to link sentences and paragraphs logically.

Vocabulary and Sentence Structure(词汇、句式及表达是否灵活多变)

Using a range of appropriate vocabulary.

Using a variety of sentence structures.

图表作文最新增加的评分标准：

最新的图表写作增加了对广大考生描述图表准确度的要求！也就是说，在以往的评分过程中，考官并不刻意要求考生描述内容的严格准确，这一点在以往的雅思考试中也不明确提出作为给分依据。但最新的雅思作文考试要求严格查看考生在语言描述过程中，是否精确地表达出图表作文给出的信息。所以大家在进行图表中数据比较、分析等过程中，培养准确解译图中信息的习惯，切忌不精确甚至错误的描述。如果这样，即使语言方面没有错误，也要被扣分。

以上是图表作文的初步介绍，后文（第二部分的第一小节）将分类阐述每类图表具体如何入手，如何达到以上评分要求的主要几点内容，帮助大家在 20 分钟内有效地完成写作任务。

1.3.2　Writing Task 2 综合说明

Present a written argument or case to an educated reader with no specialist knowledge of the following topic:

We live in a technological age. However, technology cannot solve all the world's problems. Therefore some people argue that we need to place less emphasis on technological solutions and more on other values.

To what extent do you agree or disagree with this opinion? You should use your own ideas, knowledge and experience to support your arguments with examples and relevant evidence.

对雅思 Writing Task 2 有些了解的读者可能已经意识到，上面给出的是一份典型的议论文写作题目和要求。通过这个例子，大家可以有个感性的认识，究竟 Writing Task 2 是如何出题的。不过大家要记住下面两点：

1. 要写的文章的读者是"educated reader"，所以写作风格要求比较正式（formal style）。

2. 你所写的文章不要求体现出涉及专业知识的很深的题目（"with no specialist knowledge"）。

以上面给出的题目为例，题目本身要求了两个部分：

1. 就题目展开论述：

2.必须给出你的观点。

所以在写完文章的时候,一定要问自己:我给出了我的论点了吗?

而且,最新的作文考试要求显示,如果作者能给出不同于原题陈述中的两派观点或者能给出问题(如果原文陈述的是某种问题现象)的解决方案,分数要明显高于只做简单分析然后给出自己观点的文章。

关于 Writing Task 2,在 IELTS HANDBOOK(1999)上,考试委员会给出的官方说明是这样的:

In Task 2 candidates are presented with a point of view or argument or problem.

Candidates are assessed on their ability to:

- present the solution to a problem
  (给出某个问题的解决办法)
- present and justify an opinion
  (陈述一个观点并能很好地证明)
- compare and contrast evidence, opinions and implications 含意
  (对给出的一些现象、不同的观点等进行比较、对比分析)
- evaluate and challenge ideas, evidence or argument
  (对给出的不同观点进行评价分析并给出自己的观点)

The topics are of general interest and it makes no difference what the candidate's specalist knowledge is, i.e. what their major is/was. The issues raised are interesting, suitable for and easily understood by all candidates entering postgraduate or undergraduates studies.

结合最新的考试要求动向,在这里给大家精要地阐释一下高效(高分)完成题目六步法(再具体的内容请阅读本书的第二部分的二小节。):

第一:仔细审题。并画出问题要求的几个关键点:

这一点至关重要,因为 2004 年以后,历次的考试结果和评分动向显示,考官在评分过程中严格关注考生是否完全回答了原题提到的所有内容,或者叫关键点! 如果漏掉某个关键点没有提及,评分动向显示,考生绝对得不到高分。更精确地讲,在参加今后的雅思考试中,如果考生没有完全回答原题涉及到的内容,考官很难给出高于6分的分数! 这一点十分重要,大家在仔细阅读本书后面章节的范文时,要注意体会范文是如何紧密围绕题目陈述中的几点关键展开的。但是请大家注意,范文很好地

运用同意转换技巧,用同义词或者同义表达的方式避免和原文的词汇和短语完全一致。这一方面的详细讲解在本书的后面章节中。

第二:完整地读完并理解题目,切忌粗心大意想当然。

关于这一点提示,也是考生非常容易忽视的内容。我们从多年在英国教授雅思和雅思考官的角度出发,提醒大家,每次雅思议论文的题目都是大家似曾相识的内容,但是考试出题委员会在命题过程中,每次都会增加或者删除一些关键点和要求,即使同一个话题,也可以变化成几种不同的出题题目,所以大家不要在刚看到开始的时候,就武断地认为"这个题目我写过"。一定要读完题目!

第三:确定自己的观点或者针对问题的解决方案。

这一点是雅思作文考试最新的风向标!考试委员会"厌倦"了千篇一律的简单给出观点再给出3点论据的论证文章。所以如果大家稍微拓展一下原题的两派观点而给出自己的不同观点,这样就会得到高分! 关于这一点大家要仔细阅读后面的范文!

第四:快速理顺各段主题句并列出可以用作支持论点的论据。

大家可以想好文中表达的论据,在练习纸上简练地列出,这样在写的过程中不至于忘记。

第五:最后总结要紧扣你的观点,并且牢牢记住一片完整议论文包含主要三部分:引入主题 + 正文论证 + 结论。

解读雅思作文

Goals determine what you are going to be.

目标决定你将成为什么样的人。

——*Julius Erving* 欧文

精炼，提炼

The whole of science is nothing more than the refinement of everyday thinking.

—*Albert Einstein*

爱因斯坦的名言对英文写作也颇有启示。大家学习英文文章的写作过程，是一个不断精炼语句、精炼思维的过程。本书的一个核心重点是对雅思作文系统的写作阐释和说明，帮助大家快速进入雅思写作的角色，使你的英文表达日益精炼。这一部分将大小作文分列开来，分别作系统的写作介绍。

2.1 Writing Task 1 分类讲解

2.1.1 曲线图类(Curves)

[kə:v]

曲线图是雅思小作文中比较容易写的一类图形。和其他类别的图标题目一样，写作的时候一般分为三个部分来下笔谋篇。同时下面提示的内容是在广大考生当中存在的非常普遍的疑问(时态、表达等)，这里大家可以不再困惑了。

曲线图写作结构

题目的变形

1. 引题(Introduction)

一般采用一到两句话综合介绍一下曲线图所表示的内容。第一句话一般给出图表的内容是关于什么的。如：The curve illustrates the number of cases of A-type crimes committed in the UK between the years 1990 and 2004.

注意时态。尽管原图描述的是过去的内容或者信息，但是我们这一句所说的是本图描述的信息，所以使用现在时态。开头段用一般现在时

注意千万不要照抄原文给出的相关大标题。实际上这一点也体现出雅思命题委员会对"同义转换"的强调。所以大家要切记。

第二句给出总体的曲线走势。如：

It can be seen that A-type crimes decreased dramatically to 200 cases around the middle of the 1990s and then increased to 2000 before the year 2000.

再次注意时态。这里的内容是具体发生在过去的,所以用一般过去时。

2. 正文(Describing the graph in details)

这是图表的正文部分。作为考生,要定好所要描述的内容和逻辑顺序。

3. 结尾(Concluding sentences)

可以用一到两句话结尾,但不要加自己的评论,因为加入的自己的主观意见或者看法和原图没有任何联系,所以被考官视为和主题无关(irrelevant),切记!

下面先给大家两篇曲线图的示范文章,然后我们逐步介绍细节的写作内容。

【例文 1】 改写: The line graph compares the population of smoking in males and females in the UK between 1960 and 2004. Apparently, the number of smoking for both men and women declined gradually from 1985. ↙steady

Smoking in UK

【范文 1】 line

The graph compares the population of smoking in males and females in the UK between 1960 and 2004. It is clear that the population of smoking for both men and women made a steady decrease from 1985. = decreased / declined gradually from 1985. ↙ steady

In 1960, about 700,000 men were smoking, and this number deopped gradually to 50,000 by 1974 and continued to decrease until 2004. On the contrary, the population of smoking in women in 1960 was fairly low and was about 50,000. By 1970 this figure increased to 100,000 and 200,000 in 1980. But after 1985, the number of smoking in female began to decline and continued on this downward turn until 2004.

In conclusion, the population of smoking in men and women dropped significantly throughout the period. But the smoking population of women remained lower than that of men during the entire period. (注意比较分析,注意内容表达精确)

(smoking population)

【例文2】

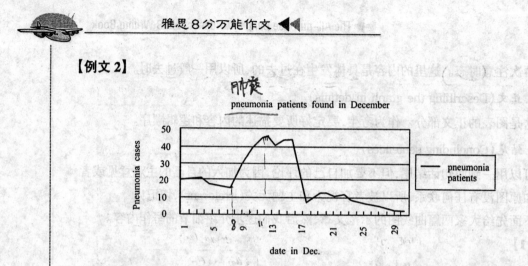

肺炎

pneumonia patients found in December

date in Dec.

【范文2】

16

The line curve above illustrates the number of patients recorded as having pneumonia on different dates in December.

During the first few days of December, the number of cases of the X disease remained steady, followed by a slight decrease before the numbers rose dramatically between the 8th and the 11th of December. The number of cases of the disease then reached a peak on the 12th, fluctuating slightly until the 15th, and then fell sharply over the following two days. There was a slight increase up to the 19th when numbers reported for the disease dropped steadily and finally reached their lowest point on the 30th of December.

[手写: ① reach the highest point at. ② peaked at 46]

Overall, the number of pneumonia patients was high between the 7th and 15th of December. It is clear that by the middle of the month, there were only a few cases of pneumonia recorded.

图中各个阶段的同义表达描述： *[手写: a gradual drop]*

1. a steady drop, a slight fall, a gradual decline, a small decrease

2. a rapid leap, a sudden rise, a marked increase, a huge growth, a dramatic rise

3. no change, a flat trend, the number remained unchanged

4. a dramatic fall, a sharp drop, a rapid plunge, a steep decline *[手写: fall dramatically]*

5. a gradual drop, a steady drop, tailing off, falling off *[手写: decline]*

下面将几种曲线图题目中经常出现的趋势作一总结。我们这里的总结特点在于给出了同义表达的交替使用。在雅思考试现场大家所能遇到的曲线图的变化不外乎这些。

曲线图常用表达

常见曲线图变化趋势	动词表达	用名词作同义替换表达
↗	rose (to)	a rise (in)
	increased (to)	an increase (in)
	went up (to)	a growth (in)
	climbed (to)	an upward trend (in)
	boomed	a boom in (a dramatic rise in)
↘	fell (to)	a decrease (in)
	declined (to)	a decline (in)
	decreased (to)	a fall (in)
	dipped (to) dropped (to)	a drop (in)
	went down (to) slumped (to)	a slump in (dramatic fall in)
	reduced (to)	a reduction (in)
→	levelled out (at)	a levelling out (of)
	did not change remained stable (at) remained steady (at) stayed constant (at) maintained the same level	a flat trend no change (in)
∧∨∧	fluctuated (around) peaked (at) plateaued (at) stood at (we use this phrase to focus on a particular point before we mention the movement, for example: in the first year, unemployment stood at…)	a fluctuation (in) reached a peak (of) reached a plateau (at)

17

一个示范例子:Aggregate output level (fell) in 2002. 可以同义转换写成:

There was a (fall) in aggregate output level in 2002.

在曲线图中表示变化程度可以用到的词汇(degree of change)

形容词	副词
dramatic	dramatically
sharp	sharply
huge	hugely
enormous	enormously
steep	steeply
substantial	substantially
considerable	considerably
significant	significantly
marked	markedly
moderate	moderately
slight	slightly
small	
minimal	minimally

在曲线图中表示变化程度可以用到的词汇(speed of change)

形容词	副词
rapid	rapidly
quick	quickly
swift	swiftly
sudden	suddenly
steady	steadily
gradual	gradually
slow	slowly

练习:我们以两个曲线图表题结束这一部分的讲解。大家写完之后按照下面的三个标准检查自己的写作是否符合高分标准。我们给出了练习2的范文,供大家再次模仿。

【曲线图作文练习 1】

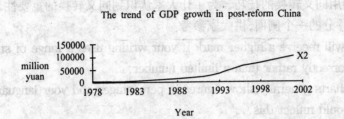

The trend of GDP growth in post-reform China

You should spend about 20 minutes on this task.

Write a report for a university lecturer describing the information in the graph below.

You should write at least 150 words.

最后,总结最新的图表作文考试高分准则:

▲是否使用了不同的方式表达图上趋势并做了精确的描述

（包括总体趋势有没有表达清楚;有无具体比较）

▲语法使用是否正确

▲词汇使用是否得当

（要求考生熟练掌握和使用我们为大家总结的同义表达）

▲句式使用有无变化

▲字数是否达到 150 以上

（注意,考官确实要清点字数。）

2.1.2　扇形图类（pie charts）

翻开每天的英文金融时报（Financial Times）或是其他经济管理类的杂志,大家就会明白为什么扇形图这么受出题委员会的青睐。扇形图是雅思小作文中考频最高的一种,经常会在考试中遇到,2004 年几次真题中的 Writing Task 1 出现的是纯扇形图。因为扇形图的自身特点,用得比较多,我们在这一小节后给大家总结了最常用的"比较"用法。

扇形图写作结构

和曲线图类相同,基本结构还是遵循引文、正文和结尾"三体"法。

开始句示范:The pie charts below illustrate the different levels of education achieved by women in China over the past three decades.

同样注意用起始句作全文的介绍,说的是图表告诉（show, illustrate, demon-

mere
adj. 仅仅的.

strate)我们什么,所以用现在时态。同时注意在第一句话中不要照搬原图表上的原话,一定要利用同义转换的技巧。为了让大家认识到同义转换的重要性,下面给出了考试委员会评分的一个侧面,供大家参考。

• You will receive a higher mark if your writing uses a range of structures and vocabulary correctly rather than a limited number...

• Pie charts generally show figures in percentages and your language in writing the report should reflect this...

【范文】

The pie charts compare the highest level of education achieved by women in China between the years 1990 and 2004. Apparently, women received a much higher level of education in China in 2004 than those women who attended schools back in 1990.

In 1990, 35% of women in China completed their elementary education and only 10% went on to university, besides which, a mere 5% of women actually completed their university studies. However, the situation in 2004 changed dramatically, in which more than half of the women in China had completed some form of higher education and among those, 25% had graduated from college with a degree with a further 30% going on to university. On the other hand, we can see that by 2004, 95% of women had received an education beyond elementary level. This is in stark contrast with the scenario in 1990.

In summary, it is obvious and noteworthy that in the 14 years from 1990 to 2004 there were many positive developments in the levels of women's education in China.

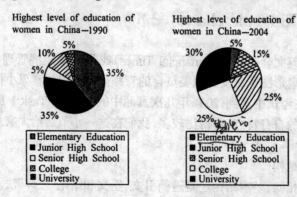

Highest level of education of women in China—1990
5% 10% 5% 5% 35% 35%

Highest level of education of women in China—2004
30% 5% 15% 25% 25%

■Elementary Education
■Junior High School
□Senior High School
◪College
■University

20

描述扇形图常用句

The highest The greatest The lowest The most The smallest	percentage of proportion of number of	men computers	are unemployed are black
Red is the Italy is the	most second most last	popular prevalent common	car colour category holiday destination

倍数的表达方式

As many Twice as many Three times as many Not as many	red cars women holiday makers	are sold are unemployed in (A) come from	as...
More Far more Much more Slightly more			than...

2.1.3   柱状图类(bar charts/columns)

在描述柱状图时,有时候使用的语言内容和曲线图类似。下面给大家一个范例。

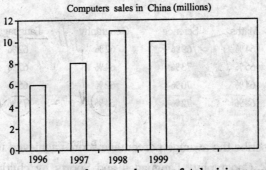

Computers sales in China (millions)

In this graph, we can see that purchases of televisions went up in 1996 and continued to rise steadily until 1998 when they dropped again slightly.

Thailand was the most popular destination for tourists from China.

一点提示：在完成这项写作任务的时候，记住你不一定要面面俱到(cover every detail)。一般情况下，需要考生选择最高或者最低的数据去比较描述。

2.1.4 表格类(tables)

表格类文章的写作和前面讲的曲线图、扇形图还有柱状图有些不同。这里没有明显的视觉感受，需要考生分析每个给出的数据。对于一些学习文科的同学或者对数字不敏感的人似乎没有优势。实际上并没有太大的困难，我们给大家示范了一篇文章，核心就是抓住表格内的"最值"数据。

【范文】

You should spend about 20 minutes on this task.

The tables below are the results of research, which examined the average percentage marks scored by boys and girls of different ages in several school subjects. Write a report for a university lecturer describing the information below. You should write a minimum of 150 words.

Boys:

Subject Age	Maths	Science	Geography	Languages	Sports
7	63%	70%	63%	62%	71%
10	65%	72%	68%	60%	74%
13	69%	74%	70%	60%	75%
15	67%	73%	64%	58%	78%

Girls:

Subject Age	Maths	Science	Geography	Languages	Sports
7	64%	69%	62%	62%	65%
10	65%	73%	64%	67%	64%
13	64%	70%	62%	65%	62%
15	68%	72%	64%	75%	60%

The tables describe the average percentage scores achieved in the school subjects of Maths, Science, Geography, Languages and Sports by children aged 7, 10, 13, and 15 based on different gender.

The subjects for which the highest average scores were recorded were Sports, at

78% (boys) and Languages, at 75% (girls). The strongest subject for each gender was revealed to be the weakest for the opposite sex, with these two subjects also comprising the lowest recorded scores, at 60% and 70% respectively. Apart from these two subjects the performance of boys and girls was comparatively similar. Although boys tended to score higher in Geography, with scores ranging from 63% to 70% and scores for girls ranged between 62% and 64%, it is obvious that both boys and girls aged 15 years old averaged scores of 64% for this subject.

To sum up, these tables offer a clear picture about the average scores achieved in five subjects by boys and girls in different age groups. (164 words)

表格写作原则：

1. 首句永远概括全部。

2. 中间永远找极值点、最值点描述。

3. 最后总结概括。

最简单的法则也往往是最有效的法则。

2.1.5 系列图表、组图、流程图类(flow charts/processes)

流程图关键是看懂图,分清逻辑关系,而用词和结构的写法与其他的图没有太大的差别。大家看下面的流程图：

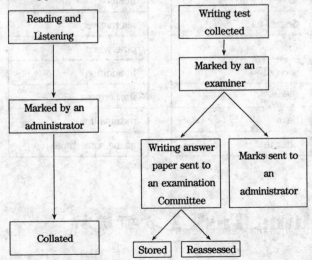

Marking procedures for English testing at the University of Manchester

这里只是一个常用的流程图的示范,考试中不管怎么变换,核心的描写思路是不变的。大家可以参考下面给出的范文体会一下。

【范文】

The flow chart illustrates the marking procedures for English language testing at the University of Manchester.

From the chart, we can see that after the papers are collected, the reading and listening papers are marked by an administrator and then collated. The writing papers, on the other hand, are treated differently. After their collection, the writing papers are marked by an external examiner. After this, the produced marks are then sent to an administrator for collation while the exam papers are sent to an examination board. The board then decides which papers need to be reassessed and which ones need to be stored.

The flow chart illustrates clearly how the English test papers are processed at the University of Manchester.

流程图的写作,审题是第一步也是非常重要的一步。在考试中如果遇到这样的题目,首先不要慌,记住,你所要写的就是按照图上所列出的内容按部就班地描述。你有可能对图中的内容并不熟悉。但是雅思考试从不测试考生对某个领域的专业知识,所以如果你有不认识的词汇,只要清楚过程,一样可以胜利完成这项写作任务。所以自信心在流程图写作中尤为重要,在看图之前就要告诉自己:我一定能写成!

流程图中常用的启承转合词汇

to begin with	finally
first of all	alternatively
first	otherwise
secondly	in addition
then	furthermore
next	meanwhile
after that	at the same time

2.2 Writing Task 2 分项讲解

Almost all of us—even if we don't do it consciously—look early in an essay for a one- or two-sentence condensation of the argument or analysis that is to follow. We refer to that condensation as a thesis statement.

The Trustees of Indiana University

2.2.1 议论文的中心主题

这一小节我们从 Writing Task 2 写作要求的核心,即"一个中心,一个主题"的要求开始,逐渐阐释如何有效地写好雅思议论文。

为了给大家一点感性的认识,对"一心一意"这个原则有一个更清楚的认知,我们先看一下雅思考试 Writing Task 2 的写作要求、测试的能力和评分标准。作者对这三项内容分别作了评述并提出了相应的解释和考生应该理解的内容。(是不是令大家想起了多年来一直耳熟能详的"考生须知"?)

25

1. Writing Task 2 的写作要求

In Writing Task 2, you will be given a discussion topic. The question will either present you with an opinion, an argument or a problem. You have to discuss all parts of the question with two or three main points and provide some supporting details for each point.

You should use your own ideas, knowledge and experience and support your arguments with examples and relevant evidence.

You have to write at least 250 words. You are advised to spend 40 minutes on this task.

在分析议论文(大作文)的写作要求之前,先送给大家一句英文,恰到好处地表达出作者的切身体会:"There are some nuances between what you think and what you are supposed to understand."也就是说,有很多同学并没有真正理解题目的要求。比如说,对于"You should use your own ideas, knowledge and experience and support your arguments with examples and relevant evidence."这句话,大家是怎么领悟的呢?在与英国的雅思考官面对面地交谈中我们发现实际上这一条要求给我们许多中国考生造成理解上的误区,在考场上拼命想自己经历过的相关事例,往往是"山穷水尽,闭门造车",在考场现去编一些例子,生硬地把"自己"加到其中。我在这里为大家解释清楚这个要求的真正含义(disabuse your misunderstanding):"using your own experience"并不是一定要大家提供自己的切身经历经验,可以是你所知道的 supporting facts, examples 等等。简而言之,大家提供和中心主旨相关的支持内容就可以,不一定要加入"I have experienced..."或者"In my experience of..."这样的内容。

2. Writing Task 2 测试的能力

This task tests your ability to do one or more of the following five points:

1. discuss a problem and present a solution
   讨论一个问题,并给出解决的方案。

2. present and justify opinions
   提出观点,加以证明。

3. compare and contrast evidence or opinions
   对比事实或者对不同的观点进行比较。

4. argue a case
   论述(证)一个事实。

5. evaluate and challenge ideas, using evidence and arguments
   对给出的不同观点作出评价。

这一部分无论以什么形式出现,主要考查考生对题目的理解和有理有据地论述思想、观点的能力。我们要做的,就是要 convince 读者,或者更确切地说是 convince 雅思考官,你的观点是强有力的!

3. 评分标准

作文的评分标准主要看考生在"观点、行文和词汇与句式"三个方面的具体表现。下面为大家具体解释。由于用英文表达评分的标准有助于大家更确切地"洞悉"考官的评判标准,所以下面的部分内容以英文的形式给出。作为一个雅思备考者,相信大家能够透彻地把握其核心意思,试试看!

Your performance in Task 2 will be assessed on the criteria below: (band 9 for candidates who demonstrate the following points)

• (观点鲜明)Arguments, and Response to the Question

1. Being able to present a clear, logical, and well-supported argument.

2. Being able to support your argument with personal experience and reasons.

3. Being able to focus on all aspects of the question and not include anything irrelevant.

对于这一点,我们前文给过简短的说明,在这里再给大家强调一下,就是 2004 年以后的考试,不仅仅要考查考生是否给出了观点,还要看考生的观点是不是能在原文提供的两种观点之上再有所延伸和拓展。所以,大家尽可能给出一种不是简单认同原文其中一种的观点。当然,对题目提及的观点内容一定要加以分析,并提出论据,论证为什么你认为你的观点更有说服力!

- (行文流畅)Progression and Clarity of Ideas

Being able to write fluently enough to make your message clear to the reader.

Being able to write cohesive sentences and paragraphs.

- (词汇句式多变)Vocabulary and Grammar

Using a range of appropriate vocabulary.

Using a variety of sentence structures.

Demonstrating good spelling and punctuation.

提醒:议论文的分数权重要大于图表作文,所以一定要重视本部分的写作内容!

关于评分标准部分的内容,下一小节(4)详细阐述如何做到"中心突出,主题鲜明",从而获得高分。而关于"句式、表达多变和行文流畅"将另分一大项详尽到位地为大家示范讲解。之所以这样做的原因就是要在规定的时间内完成一篇优秀的雅思议论文,必须首先把握它的评分标准,有的放矢地进行训练,改进自己的不足,完善自己的写作能力。下面阐述全书强调的"一心一意"(中心突出,主题鲜明)的写作原则。

27

4.关于中心主题

所谓"一心一意"(中心突出,主题鲜明),就是指一篇好的雅思议论文,只能论述"一个中心,一个主题",不得有一句和主题不相关的内容,给出的 supporting examples and facts 也丝毫不能脱离你所论述的中心主旨(thesis)。关于中心主旨要惟一(one thesis)这个话题,大家如果翻看专业书籍,都会有详细的讲解,甚至有整本的关于这个内容的书,但是我们不建议大家先翻看理论,再回到雅思议论文的写作训练中来,那样就走了弯路。下面的阐释和例子分析会给大家一个明确的认识。

首先说一下"观点鲜明"(Arguments, Ideas and Evidence)这一项。这一项是雅思考试考官最关注的内容,言外之意,也就是占据最多的分数点。下面给大家两篇学生的习作,大家先快速浏览一遍,然后评估一下哪一篇文章应该得高一点的分数。(这两篇文章都源自曼彻斯特大学培训研究生助教课程中,示范如何给学生的习作评分的材料,资料出处在本书参考文献中给出。)

【文章1】①

Environmental Epidemiology

Consider the evidence that bathing in the sea in Britain is harmful to health.

Pollution of the sea has been a long-standing environmental issue and there have been many studies done on this subject. Until the 1990s sewage was allowed to be

---

① 这两篇文章均摘自曼彻斯特大学"2003~2004年研究生助教培训——如何给学生作文评分"部分的材料(Assessing students' essays)。文章稍长,请大家主要看它们各自有没有中心论点,论据是不是围绕某个明确的中心(thesis)展开的。

dumped untreated into British waters and even now primary treatment can only kill 30 ~ 80% of bacteria and viruses. Secondary treatment is more successful and can kill 99% — the remaining being left to float around in the sea.

Even on Britain's so-called 'Blue flag' beaches human sewage can be seen. Often the problem is that the sewage pipes end close to the shore so sewage is washed back onto the beaches.

Government legislation is relatively weak — in the USA it is 20 times stronger.

EC Directive regulations are based on coliform bacteria presented in samples. Presence of coliform can indicate the presence of faecal deposits in the water and pathogens may be present.

The use of coliform as an indication of pollution is not very helpful as it has a relatively short life in the sea as it is a bacteria which can be easily killed.

Regulations are also based on 'out-of-date' disease measures of such things as typhoid, polio — possibly caused by water pollution/contamination.

Regulation fails to take account of more minor infections such as ear, nose and throat infections, gastro enteritis and other stomach upsets. A more useful guideline to the presence of pollutants in sea water would be to use the presence of enterococci which is not so easily destroyed and consequently appears to be a more reliable method than coliform bacteria. An additional problem with British coastal areas is that tests take time to complete so the tests are never a true indicator of current pollution levels. Also as the bacteria are so easily killed results vary in different parts of the sea.

An important epidemiological study on this subject was carried out by Cabelli in the United States of America. It was Cabelli who indicated that enterococci was a more reliable indicator of pollution levels.

This study was a prospective cohort study in which he divided people into bathers and non-bathers and did follow up questionnaires on their health. He concluded that bathing in sea water had definite effects on the health of bathers — particularly for gastroenteritis symptoms which increased significantly in bathers, and also other minor infections such as ear, eye, nose and throat problems.

Cabelli's study was particularly important as British epidemiologists based their studies on his.

One such study was carried out by Balarajan in Ramsgate using a 'Cabelli' type of study design. He recruited bathers and non-bathers and did detailed analysis on their health and found similar results to Cabelli. Although Balarajan found stronger evidence for gastro enteritis and diaroaha after exposure to sea water.

However both Cabelli and Balarajan studies are subject to bias and confounders so caution is needed in interpreting these results. For example, there may have been bias in reporting symptoms — interviewer or response bias. Also subjects were self-selecting as to bathers and non-bathers so there may have been selection bias. Stricter control over health reporting symptoms would also have been beneficial. There should also have been stricter measurement of water samples as these were not done at different depths, etc. However, both of these studies indicated a positive relationship between bathing water and adverse health effects — along with other studies done on other British beaches.

Perhaps a more useful and reliable study was the one undertaken by Kay et al. This was a more well designed randomised controlled trial on the effects of British bathing water quality and health in Britain. It was carried out on 4 UK resorts over 4 summers and cost over 1 million.

They used students for this study — the study was large (over 1000) and time consuming. The people were split into bathers and non-bathers. The non-bathers were contained on the beach in a roped-off section. Bathers were asked to spend at least 10 minutes in the water and to completely submerge themselves (including their head) at least 3 times.

Sample of water were taken at different height levels in bathing areas and both coliform bacteria and presence of enteroccoci and streptococci were measured.

All participants underwent intense interviewing of the health, diet habits and other possible confounders while on the beach. Present health was recorded and follow-up interviews were carried out at one and again at three weeks to discover any possible adverse health effects or infections.

The study concluded that there was a significant relationship between bathers and gastro enteritis and diaroaha symptoms — 31% higher symptoms in bathers than non-bathers.

Although ear, throat, nose and eye infections were higher results were not very significant for these.

The study also found a positive relationship between depth of bathing and pres-

29

ence of symptoms (this was also found in other studies e.g. Cabelli, Balarajan were 'paddlers' had less symptoms than 'swimmers', etc.)

An important point is that all of these studies (and others) showed a relationship between bathing and sea water — all indicated an increase in minor symptoms, especially stomach upsets, with bathing in sea water. Consequently this consistency must be taken as a positive indicator that bathing in the sea is probably harmful to health, although it can't actually prove it!

However the many studies undertaken all point to the same conclusion and people are increasingly wary about bathing in the sea and are relying on beach guides e.g. Blue Flag beaches, etc. as indicators of cleaner beaches — but if based on coliform bacteria are not really reliable guides either!

It is also probably worth noting that the Kay et al. study involved students — there may have been an even larger (more significant) result if children had been used as they are more susceptible to minor infections.

【文章2】

Environmental Epidemiology

Consider the evidence that bathing in the sea in Britain is harmful to health.

In Britain there are different methods for treating sewage in different places. In some treatment works the effluent is cleaned and returned to water supplies to be reused. It has been estimated that water from the Thames may have passed through 20 people!

However in many places which have access to the coast councils have opted to discharge sewage to the sea after only limited treatment. Sewage outfalls vary in length and should ideally only be sited after extensive surveying into current flow so that effluent is diluted and dispersed away from the coast.

Concern arose about pollution caused by sewage and in 1959 the Department of Public Health undertook a survey which found no connection with diseases such as polio, typhoid and smallpox. It concentrated only on major diseases and ignored any gastrointestinal illnesses. Since then the volume of discharges has increased dramatically. Evidence of increase from the domestic sector includes daily bathing and showering, use of automatic washing machines and dishwashers, as opposed to the 1950s when washing clothes tended to be a weekly event rather than daily.

The cleanliness of beaches and quality of sea bathing water has become increasingly more important over the last decade, especially since EEC directives pass or fail beaches according to their fitness for leisure pursuits.

Sea water quality is measured by the coliform count or the e. coli count. If the sea water exceeds a set limit in parts per thousand it fails the test. Fairly recently in Wales only 4 out of 26 beaches passed the tests.

However, using coliform counts as a mark of excellence can be deceptive as they can vary even from hour to hour, take several hours for analysis to take place and may not be uniformly dispersed through the water depending on current flow.

In 1989 Cabelli et al (USA) undertook a study in which bathers were approached on a beach and asked to participate in the survey.

Questions were asked about health, whether they swam, paddled or sat in the sun and they gave telephone numbers where they were contacted a week later to see if any ill effects had occurred. Coliform and e. coli was measured at the time of swimming. This study showed a link between sea bathing in raised coliform counts and gastrointestinal and ear/eye infections.

However this study had its imperfections as some of the participants were paid to take part.

Basically it has a good study design though and has been repeated in Great Britain. A similar survey was carried out in Blackpool when a number of children were included in the survey.

There are confounders such as the consumption of ice-creams on the beach, eating hot-dogs, burgers or even home made picnics which may have gone slightly off in the sun. There may also be recall bias about children swimming. Another survey was carried out near Ramsgate where a cohort of students was used. They were designated as bathers, paddlers, or sun-bathers and questioned a week later about ill effects. Coliform counts taken through the day. An association between raised coliform counts and gastrointestinal infections and ear/eye irritation was found.

第二篇文章虽然文笔上似乎逊色于第一篇文章,而且内容似乎也不如首篇的充实,但是我们找不到第一篇文章的明显的中心主题(thesis),所以实际上第二篇 Essay 得到了较高的分数。这个例子生动地说明,我们在写雅思议论文的时候,如果没有给出一个鲜明的主题,即使文采再好,也得不了高分。"形散神不散"的中式散文,千万不能应用于英文文章的写作。

你的中心主旨一般都要通过一句全文主题句给出。看下面的例子,这是一段标准的雅思 Writing Task 2 的开始段：

Since the dawn of 21st century, science has become an increasingly specialised and compartmentalised subject. Some people propose that science will not provide amateurs any room to stay. Perhaps surprisingly, however, amateurs are still important.

上面这段话是非常常见的雅思议论文的开始段落，原题题干可以这样来问：

Since the beginning of this century, amateurs have been playing fewer and fewer roles in scientific areas. Some people think that science will not need amateurs any more. To what extent do you agree or disagree with this statement?

You should use your own ideas, knowledge and experience and support your arguments with examples and relevant evidence.

You have to write at least 250 words. You are advised to spend 40 minutes on this task.

似乎这是一种八股式的老套文章，而从示范的首段大家可能已经看出，最后一句"Perhaps surprisingly, however, amateurs are still important."给出了全文的中心主旨，那就是"业余爱好者在科学这个领域中仍然重要"。这样一段简单明快的开始段落，还隐含了雅思考试中(听、说、读、写)所常用的另外一条技巧：同义转换。关于这一点在后续的内容中会有详细的说明，在这一部分我们主要体会一下"一心一意"这个原则。在"观点鲜明"这一要求里面，第三点"Being able to focus on the topic and not include anything irrelevant"所要求的核心就是这个意思。在中文作文里面，我们可以这样描述：

五月时节，四处一片盎然生机。这春天给了我们无限的动力，会让人们不禁想起了"五岳归来不看山，黄山归来不看岳"的雄壮。是啊，黄山，集泰山之雄伟、华山之险峻、恒山之烟云、庐山之飞瀑、雁荡之巧石、峨眉之秀丽于一体，尤以奇松、怪石、云海、温泉四绝闻名天下，让华夏儿女为之骄傲！想我们的祖国，壮丽河山，奇域凌峰，无处不美！再看今天祖国的科技发展，更是让世人刮目相看。我认为，中国这样伟大，一定会在下个世纪成为经济强国。为什么这样说呢，我们可以看下面三点理由……

在练习写雅思议论文之前，很多同学虽然有着不同的英文写作经验，但是往往比较容易受到母语的干扰，从上面一段话就可以体现出来。应该说上文的文采可圈可点，颇有几分豪气，开始的"铺垫"也是很有力度。但是，如果我们在写一篇雅思议论文的时候，在已给定"Some people propose that the economy in China will boom in this century. Do you agree or disagree with this view?"作为 topic 的情况下，也以和上段中文同样的手法去写，恐怕就做不到"一心一意"，也就是说达不到"主题鲜明"的评分标准的要求了。为什么呢？因为如果这样写，考官的第一印象是"The sentences are irrelevant to the topic, and to the thesis."我们常说"良好的开端是成功的一半"，其实反过来说，"不好的开头是失败的前奏"。这句话的含义我们可以在雅思写作考试中体会得淋漓尽致。

对于"Being able to present a clear, logical, well-supported argument"这个要求，其实质仍然要求大家做到围绕"一个中心，一个主题"的原则来进行布局谋篇。如何才能做到"well-supported"呢？要求大家所给的"support"内容，一定要能够很好地证明你的主题，千万不能出现和主题不相关的句子。大家看下面这个例子：

Since the dawn of 20th century, cars have been a symbol of the modernization and civilization. The debate over the pros and cons of inventions like the car are representative of the type of questions raised concerning advancements in break-through technologies that affect modern societies. Although there are some negligible disadvantages, the advantages of the car, in my view, far outweigh the disadvantages.

......

Another advantage of cars is that they also contribute to economic development. The car industry plays a positive role in the development of economy. <u>Last year, the total income in many countries increased due to expansions in the car manufacturing sector. Perhaps everybody can feel this kind of economic boom.</u>

这篇文章的开始段落很好，引入主题之后非常明快地给出中心主题，也就是作者的观点（cars provide more advantages than disadvantages）。问题出在第二段话的画线部分，大家仔细体会一下，这句话与"cars"的好处不相关，也就不能很好地论证你的中心主题（thesis）。在评卷人眼里，第一项评分标准就打了折扣。而我们稍作修改就可以了：

......

Another advantage of cars is that they also contribute to economic development. The car industry plays a positive role in the development of economy. *According to a recent report, there are over one million cars that are produced and sold each year in America and the income from this accounts for 30 per cent of the U. S. GDP. Undoubtedly, the profits from car industries make up an enormous part of any economy.*

......

斜体部分的内容充实详尽地证明了确实"cars contribute a lot to economic development"。其中的"report"，"30 per cent"都和这段话的分论点主题句（第一句）紧

33

密相关,没有丝毫脱离。从这个例子大家可以总结出来,在我们每写一句话的时候,都要问自己"这句话和主题思想(中心)真的相关吗?"如果回答是肯定的,你就做到了这一项的要求。

"主题鲜明"部分涉及到的另一个非常重要的内容就是"中心主题(thesis)"的陈述或者给出。在雅思议论文的写作中,考生一定要给出你的观点(thesis),这也是雅思作文写作中最重要的一项。实际上在英文写作中,我们把一篇文章的中心句(thesis sentence/statement)比喻成一把大伞(umbrella statement),所有的论述内容(分论点、支持的例子等等)都必须能被它所覆盖(cover)。

为了有效地理解 thesis (sentence)——议论文的中心主题是成功完成雅思 Writing Task 2 的关键。请阅读我们给大家提供的 2 段关于这一点的英文解释①,一定要仔细体会一下:

1. Focusing Your Thesis (一切内容围绕中心展开)

"A thesis can be clearly defined and still lead to a rambling essay if it is not adequately focused. A good thesis narrows your topic to an idea that you can successfully develop within the framework of your essay. From the general topic of health hazards, you might propose a thesis such as, 'The average American is exposed to many health hazards.' This thesis, though clearly defined, is so broad that you would never be able to cover it adequately in a short essay. You would wind up either jumping from one health hazard to another, discussing each only superficially, or zeroing in on one or two health hazards and, thus, failing to demonstrate your own thesis. A more narrowly focused thesis, such as "The Constitution of the United States should be amended to prohibit the production and sale of cigarettes," commits you to an idea that you can carefully analyze and defend in four or five pages."

2. Supporting Your Thesis (支持你的中心论点)

"A good thesis should be well supported. This requirement in IELTS Writing Task 2 might more properly be considered a requirement of the essay you wrote as a whole. In any case, if the essay is to be effective—if it is to persuade readers of your thesis, or at least of your credibility—you must provide arguments that are cogent and numerous enough to satisfy the critical readers or more precisely, to cater for IELTS examiners, and you must go on to support your arguments with facts and examples centering on your thesis."

---

① 以下两段引用内容出自 The Writing Centre, by Craig Waddell:http://www.rpi.edu/web/writingcenter/thesis.html

如何快速有效地表达中心主题句

接下来一个自然的问题就是：IELTS Writing Task 2 中的中心主题句是如何来写出来的呢？虽然主题句的给出看起来并不难，但是我们在教学过程中见过许多学生在实际写作中却经常遇到问题。大家看下面的一句话(假定"You are writing an essay for a class on fitness, and you might be asked to choose a popular weight-loss product to evaluate.")这是一位雅思备考者写的，或许你也写过同样的"问题"主题句：There are some negative and positive aspects to the Chinese green tea.

这不是一个有效的主题句，因为它并没有给出观点(stand)。记住，我们不能在作文中写"……既好又坏"，这样的句子在考官眼里是模糊的表达(vague expression)。怎么改呢？

Because Chinese green tea promotes rapid weight loss that results in the loss of muscle and lean body mass, it poses a potential danger to customers.

改完之后就是一个非常有效的中心主题句，因为它给出了你的观点。顺便说一下，一些考生习惯了用"I think..."等形式来表达自己的观点句子，而实际上像上一句的例子，"it poses a potential danger to customers"就给出了你的观点，不一定要出现"我认为……"这样的内容。进一步说，实际上英文书面语中表达个人观点常用"I believe...""I propose..."等等，而很少用"I think..."这些形式，希望大家能够学会我们给出的这种地道用法。(尽管口语里我们可以用"I think"这样的方式陈述。)

中心句子的给出，还有一个常见失误就是你的句子里给出了不止一个"中心"，由于是英文的表达，中国考生经常犯这方面的错误。事实胜于雄辩，看看先面这个例子你能不能分辨出它的毛病①？

"Companies need to exploit the marketing potential of the Internet, and web pages can provide both advertising and customer support."

这又是一个不得分的主题句陈述。为什么呢？因为这句话本身所传递的意思让考官无法断定这篇文章是关于"marketing on the Internet"还是关于"web pages"的(这两者是不同的)。

但是如果稍作改动，就可以达到很好的"主题鲜明，一心一意"的要求(为什么?)

"Because the Internet is filled with tremendous marketing potential, companies should exploit this potential by using web pages that offer both advertising and customer support."

---

① 出自"Essay Writing Centre: http://essayinfo.com/basics/thesis.php".

35

好，现在大家一定已经有了如何写好中心主题句的概念，关于行文流畅和句式表达多变是我们下一项要给大家讲解的内容。

2.2.2 关于句式、表达多变和行文流畅

1. 句式、表达多变——"同义转换"的魔力（A Powerful Tool）

作者小时候曾看到过一块宣传牌，上面写的"一切为了人民群众，为了一切人民群众，为了人民群众的一切"。同样的道理，我想这样说："一切为了雅思考生；为了一切雅思考生；为了雅思考生的一切。"

这里想给大家揭示的就是句式多变的方法和其本身的语言魅力。

这是第一点启示，而另外更重要的一点是，大家可能已经发现上面三个排比句子表达的意思很相近，只是做了句式上的一点点改动，也就是我们所强调的、雅思考试无处不在的"同义转换"。下面是《剑桥雅思系列》（Cambridge IELTS 3）听力练习第一课 Section One 中的一个对话原文和原文练习题目：相关的原文对白部分（tapescript）：

Janice: Hello...Flagstone.

Jon: Oh, hello. Is that Flagstone Properties?

Janice: Yes, that's right. *Flagstone here*. How can I help you?

Jon: Hello. I'm ringing just to make enquiries about renting a house. My name's Jon Anderson.

......

Janice: Right, what sort of price were you thinking of?

Jon: Well, could you give me some idea?

Janice: Certainly. It really ranges from £250 per month.

Jon: Only £250?

Janice: Yes, to about £*500* depending on a number of different factors.

Jon: What does it depend on?

Janice: Well, obviously the quality of the area. And *then whether there's a garden*.

Jon: Well, as I said, we'd want a garden.

Janice: And *a garage* pushes up the price

......

【问题】

Section 1

Complete the notes below.

Example   **Answer**

Name of agent   <u>Flagstone</u>

Areas deal with: (1)_____

Rent: from (2)_____ to _____ a month

Depends on: the area

                       availability of (3)_____

                       garage

很明显,填空题的(3):availability of _____的答案应该是 garden,对应原文对白中的斜体字。[(1)和(2)的答案也是对应的另外两处斜体字部分。]

以上一个例子和几点说明是用听力中出现的内容作点拨的,雅思阅读理解中的同义转换现象就更是无处不在了。我们用 *IELTS PLUS* 一书中第一套题的阅读理解文章 "In Praise of Amateurs"("赞扬业余爱好者")的第一道文章缩写填空(summary)题目和对应的原文部分做个示范。以后大家运用这里讲过的知识再去浏览在国内读者见得比较多的《剑桥雅思系列 1、2、3》(Cambridge IELTS 1,2,3)① 中的文章,或者是任何一篇英文文章,都会体会到这种精彩的"同义转换考试技巧"的魔力!

【例文】

In Praise of Amateurs

During the scientific revolution of the 17th century, scientists were largely men of private means who pursued their interest in natural philosophy for their own edification. **<u>Only in the past century or two</u>** has it become possible to make a living from investigating the workings of nature. Modern science was, in other words, built on the work of amateurs. Today, science is an increasingly specialised and compartmentalised subject, the domain of experts who know more and more about less and less. Perhaps surprisingly, however, amateurs - even those without private means - are still important.

---

① 《剑桥雅思系列》是国内书架最常见的雅思书目,其选材、模式等都遵循以往的雅思考试形式。惟一的遗憾是如果单使用这套教材备考,会在真正考试中发现这套题目的难度稍微低一些,而《IELTS PLUS》这本书难度却是非常合适。更加巧合的是,在 IELTS PLUS 出版之后,竟然出现几次听力考试的内容与书中内容完全相同的情况(2004 年春季期间)。虽然本书不能完全代替 IELTS PLUS,但是读者可以基本上得到全部的核心思想。

A recent poll carried out at a meeting of the American Association for the Advancement of Science by astronomer Dr Richard Fienberg found that, in addition to his field of astronomy, amateurs are actively involved in such fields as acoustics, horticulture, ornithology, meteorology, hydrology and palaeontology. Far from being crackpots, amateur scientists are often in close touch with professionals, **some of whom rely heavily on their co-operation.**

Admittedly, some fields are more open to amateurs than others. Anything that requires expensive equipment is clearly a no-go area. And some kinds of research can be dangerous: "most amateur chemists", joked Dr Fienberg, "are either locked up or have blown themselves to bits". But amateurs can make valuable contributions in fields from rocketry to palaeontology and the rise of the Internet has made it easier than ever before to collect data and distribute results.

Exactly which field of study has benefited most from the contributions of amateurs is a matter of some dispute. Dr Fienberg makes a strong case for astronomy. There is, he points out, a long tradition of collaboration between amateur and professional sky watchers. Numerous comets, asteroids and even the planet Uranus were discovered by amateurs. Today, in addition to comet and asteroid spotting, amateurs continue to do valuable work observing the brightness of variable stars and detecting novae - "new" stars in the Milky Way and supernovae in other galaxies. Amateur observers are helpful, says Dr Fienberg, because there are so many of them (they far outnumber professionals) and **because they are distributed all over the world.** This makes special kinds of observations possible: if several observers around the world accurately record the time when a star is eclipsed by an asteroid, for example, it is possible to derive useful information about the asteroid's shape.

Another field in which amateurs have traditionally played an important role is palaeontology. Adrian Hunt, a palaeontologist at Mesa Technical College in New Mexico, insists that his is the field in which amateurs have made the biggest contribution. Despite the development of high-tech equipment, he says, the best sensors for finding fossils are human eyes - lots of them. Finding volunteers to look for fossils is not difficult, he says, **because of the near-universal interest in anything to do with dinosaurs.** As well as helping with this research, volunteers learn about science, a process he calls "recreational education".

Rick Bonney of the Cornell Laboratory of Ornithology in Ithaca, New York, con-

38

tends that amateurs have contributed the most in his field. There are, he notes, thought to be as many as 60 million birdwatchers in America alone. Given their huge numbers and the wide geographical coverage they provide, Mr Bonney has enlisted thousands of amateurs in a number of research projects. Over the past few years their observations have uncovered previously unknown trends and cycles in bird migrations and revealed declines in the breeding populations of several species of migratory birds, prompting a habitat conservation programme.

Despite the successes and whatever the field of study, collaboration between amateurs and professionals is not without its difficulties. Not everyone, for example, is happy with the term "amateur". Mr Bonney has coined the term "citizen scientist" because he felt that other words, such as "volunteer" sounded disparaging. A more serious problem is the question of how professionals can best acknowledge the contributions made by amateurs. Dr. Fienberg says that some amateur astronomers are happy to provide their observations but grumble about not being reimbursed for out-of-pocket expenses. Others feel let down when their observations are used in scientific papers, but they are not listed as co-authors. Dr. Hunt says some amateur palaeontologists are disappointed when told that they cannot take finds home with them.

These are legitimate concerns but none seems insurmountable. Provided amateurs and professionals agree the terms on which they will work together beforehand, there is no reason why co-operation between the two groups should not flourish. Last year Dr. S. Carison, founder of the Society for Amateur Scientists, won an award worth $290,000 for his work in promoting such co-operation. He says that one of the main benefits of the prize is the endorsement it has given to the contributions of amateur scientists, which has done much to silence critics among those professionals who believe science should remain their exclusive preserve.

At the moment, says Dr. Carison, the society is involved in several schemes including an innovative rocket-design project and the setting up of a network of observers who will search for evidence of a link between low-frequency radiation and earthquakes. The amateurs, he says, provide enthusiasm and talent, while the professionals provide guidance "so that anything they do discover will be taken seriously". Having laid the foundations of science, amateurs will have much to contribute to its ever-expanding edifice.

Summary

Prior to the 19th century, professional __1__ did not exist and scientific research was largely carried out by amateurs. However, while __2__ today is mostly the domain of professionals, a recent US survey highlighted the fact that amateurs play an important role in at least seven __3__ and indeed many **professionals are reliant on their __4__**. In areas such as astronomy, amateurs can be invaluable when making specific __5__ on a global basis. Similarly in the area of palaeontology their involvement is invaluable and helpers are easy to recruit because of the popularity of __6__. Amateur birdwatchers also play an active role and their work has led to the establishment of a __7__. Occasionally the term "amateur" has been the source of disagreement and alternative names have been suggested but generally speaking, as long as the professional scientists __8__ the work of the non-professionals, the two groups can work productively together.

【答案】

1. scientists   2. science   3. fields   4. co-operation
5. observations 6. dinosaurs 7. programme 8. acknowledge

【解析】

下面解释主要表明如何定位到问题所在部分的英文表达和原文部分的陈述是同义转换，这样，就可以很快很准地找到定位处。

- 填空题中表述的"**Prior to the 19th century**" = 原文中的"**Only in the past century or two**"提供的信息。从而定位到 __1__ 的答案应该是 scientists。

- **professionals are reliant on their __4__** = 原文中的"**some of whom rely heavily on their co-operation.**"答案应该是 co-operation。

- invaluable when making specific __5__ on a global basis. = 对应原文中的"**because they are distributed all over the world.**"找到这个地方(文章粗体字部分)，自然很快地就会定位到 observation 是答案。

- recruit because of the popularity of __6__. = **because of the near-universal interest in anything to do with dinosaurs.**大家看，popularity(受欢迎的)不就是 near-universal interest 的同义转换表达吗？答案自然就是 dinosaurs①。

---

① Dinosaur 意思是"恐龙"。关于这样的单词如何记忆以及更多的同义词表达和记忆方法，请参阅《雅思同义词词汇必备》，张成思，大连理工大学出版社。那是该书的姊妹篇，大家结合使用，会更有效地提高词汇和写作能力。

也就是说,如果大家在熟悉了雅思的这种同义转换现象,在阅读理解中可以很快地定位(locate)到答案所在原文的近似位置,从而准确快速地填对答案。

最后,我们回到雅思写作当中来。实际上,我们稍微想一想就可以明白写作和阅读理解是一回事。有写出来的文章,才谈得上之后读者或者是考生的阅读,也就才涉及到阅读理解能力等等的说法。雅思 A 类写作即学术类(Academic)写作,要求写出来的文章是比较正式的文体。为了深刻体会写作中的同义转换的重要性和必要性,我们看下面这篇由卡耐基梅隆大学 Tepper 商学院的著名货币经济学家 McCallum (Carnegie Mellon University - David A. Tepper School of Business)写的一篇议论文的片断,体会一下无处不在的同义转换。

...The purpose of our study is to consider several methodological issues relevant for study of the monetary transmission process. These issues involve relative emphasis on monetary shocks **as opposed to** systematic policy adjustments; vector autoregression vs. structural modelling research strategies...

这里 as opposed to 等同于 vs. (versus 的缩写形式),为了避免重复,作者用了同意表达的技巧。

大家再看一个典型的雅思作文片断:

The appearance of cars has caused many social problems. What is your opinion?

...I believe cars have indeed caused many problems in society and we need to reduce the use of cars.

First of all, we must consider the severe traffic caused by cars...

Another consideration is that cars generate serious pollution...

Admittedly, cars facilitate our travel and make people's daily commute much easier than before. However, the adverse effects of cars significantly outweigh the benefits they bring.

...

这里表现的实际是非常常见的一种同义转换现象,就是不同词性的转换使用来表达相同的意思。动词 consider 与 another consideration 的交换使用显得作者写作技巧成熟,也使得文章不单调重复,也只有这样的文章才符合考官的口味,才能赢得高分!

在学术类写作中,同义转换表达之常见从以下几段小文章可见一斑。以下都是经典的雅思作文范文的节选,请仔细体会模仿。

41

【范文 1】

Any government, whether rich or poor, cannot put every penny into education, even though it may be trying to improve overall conditions for education and to create much needed rewards for teachers. Private schools, on the other hand, help to narrow government spending on education by charging wealthy students expensive tuition fees in return for superior learning facilities and highly sought after staff. That is why the governments throughout the world, whether developed or developing, encourage individuals and enterprises to establish private schools. The Chinese government has even put forward an incentive to support any interested parties, both in China and from overseas, to help promote and expand existing private education across the country.

【解析】

rich 和 wealthy 近义。

【范文 2】

Firstly, modern people suffer from greater tension so that they have less time to communicate with each other. More and more people are living in urban areas, where life has a quick rhythm. Due to fierce competition, city dwellers have to be hardworking in order to keep up with the pace of city life. Everybody is busy all the time and the ever increasing pressures at work deprive us of a casual way of life. Moreover, living in apartments in isolated blocks, we are becoming more and more removed from each other. And more often than not, it is no longer convenient for us to meet one another freely.

【解析】

tensions 表达了和 pressures 完全相同的意思,但是这样写就不会显得单调重复;画线部分也是一种巧妙的同意改写形式: have less time to communicate with each other,意思就是 are isolated from each other。但是应用了同义转换表达立刻给文章添色增辉!

【范文 3】①

Activities in environments that pose great danger to humans, such as locating sunken ships, cleanup of nuclear waste, prospecting for underwater mineral deposits, and active volcano **exploration**, are ideally suited to robots. Similarly, robots can ex-

① 出自"Uses for Robots", George A. Bekey, B.S., M.S., Ph.D.

42

plore distant planets. NASA's Galileo, an unpiloted space probe, travelled to Jupiter in 1996 and performed tasks such as determining the chemical content of the atmosphere there.

【解析】

名词 exploration 与动词 explore 交错使用,达到简洁却又非常有效的同义转换效果!

总之,在雅思写作中,一定要学会并能够灵活运用这种百试不爽的"同义转换"技巧! 想一想,在现实生活中,你愿意和一个说话总是重复一种老套模式的人交谈吗? 你能欣赏一个反复重复着"社会发展很快"的演讲者吗? 至少我们也期望他(她)能用一下"巨大的腾飞"这样的替换,是不是? 从这个角度讲,就很容易理解为什么如果你能运用"同义转换"雅思考官会给你一个好分数了! A powerful tool, isn't it!

2. 行文如流水,文章方流畅——雅思作文高分要诀(The Key to High Marks)   43

古人讲究"行文流水击节而歌,杏花巷里沽酒饯行"。文人墨客更讲求"对月吟诗句,对镜饮长虹。""弹琴酌酒喜堪俦,几案婷婷点缀幽。隔座香分三径露,抛书人对一枝秋。" 只有行文如流水,写出的文章才能彰显流畅。而英文写作所要求的不是那种"霜前月下谁家种,槛外篱边何处秋"的委婉,英语作文要求思路清晰,文章的脉络一目了然,讲究的是很强的逻辑性。这些特点和要求在学术类雅思作文中显得尤为突出。这就要求我们能遵循简洁而不是简单(concise but not simple)并有逻辑的布局谋篇。

那么如何做到雅思作文的"行文流水"呢? 最好的解说就是用原汁原味的文章给大家示范。下面我们用一段非常常见的雅思议论文片断和一篇由哈佛大学的著名经济学家① 曼昆(Gregory Mankiw, Professor of Economics at Harvard University)写的短文章:What Macroeconomists Study 作例子。

1)一个小段落②

Avoiding pollution can be a full-time job. **Try not to inhale** traffic fumes; **keep away** from chemical plants and building-sites; **wear** a mask when cycling. **It is enough** to make you want to stay at home. **But that**, according to a growing body of scientific evidence, would also be a bad idea. **Research shows** that levels of pollutants such as hazardous gases, particulate matter and other chemical "nasties" are usually higher

---

① 有的读者可能会有这样的疑问:"为什么经常以经济学家的文章示范?"有两个原因,第一个原因是各类学科的学术型人物写出来的文章都符合典型雅思作文的套路层次,只是文章深度、长度不同罢了。所以即使举教育学专业的人写的文章,效果也是一样的。另一个原因是经济学家是世界上两大思维最敏捷的人之一(另一类是哲学家),所以他们写出的文章逻辑性非常强,有很强的借鉴作用。

② 节选自《IELTS PLUS》,2002。

indoors than out, even in the most polluted cities. **Since** the average American spends 18 hours indoors for every hour outside, it looks as though many environmentalists may be attacking the wrong target.

这段话第一句陈述一个论断,然后紧接着用3个并列的动作(动词短语来实现)加以阐释。接着用指代词"it"衔接前文提到的内容。接下去用转折连词 but 做一个小转折,最后用一个"since"呈现出一个因果关系来(Since the average American spends 18 hours indoors for every hour outside, it looks as though many environmentalists may be attacking the wrong target.)。整段文章非常紧凑,搭配合理,衔接自然紧密,逻辑清晰,用词多变,是具有代表性的"星级"段落。这就是我们要达到的理想的雅思作文。

2)一篇完整的文章

The New Output-Inflation Trade-off

One of the hallmarks(特点) of economic analysis is the recognition that choice involves trade-offs. Whether it's a consumer deciding if the roominess of a sports utility vehicle is worth the lower gas mileage, or a firm deciding whether lower wages of an overseas production facility compensate for the lower worker productivity, or Congress deciding whether a new expenditure program justifies the higher taxes needed to finance it, trade-offs must be faced. The same is true in the conduct of monetary policy. Acting too slowly to head off inflation may risk an increase in expected inflation that will make subsequent moves to reduce inflation more costly, while acting too quickly may run the risk of slowing economic growth prematurely.

Remark1:首段用"经济分析的公认特点是承认各种平衡关系的存在(one of the hallmarks of economic analysis is the recognition that choice involves trade-offs.)"引入主题陈述内容——货币政策的贯彻实施(The same is true in the conduct of monetary policy.),继而暗示出作者主题观点:实施货币政策的过程也要平衡好产出与通货膨胀率之间的关系。

During the 1960s and early 1970s, many economists and policymakers believed a central bank could achieve permanently lower unemployment by accepting permanently higher inflation. Attempts to exploit such a trade-off to gain the benefits of lower unemployment were, unfortunately, self-defeating(自欺欺人的). As unemployment fell and inflation rose, individuals began to expect that inflation would be higher. Workers demanded more rapidly rising money wages to compensate for expected price increases, and firms were willing to agree to these wage demands as they expected to be able to pass through their increased costs by raising prices. Rather than remaining stable at a new higher level, the inflation rate continued to increase as long as unemployment remained below the economy's natural rate. That experience has convinced most policymakers that no such trade-off exists. Instead, most agree that the average level of the unemployment rate and the long-run rate of real economic growth are determined by such fundamentals as technological change, population growth, labor market institutions, and the skills of the work force. These factors are unrelated to the economy's average rate of inflation, so allowing average inflation to rise brings no long-run benefit in the form of faster growth or lower average unemployment.

　　Remark2:具体分析中央银行(central bank)应该如何正确认识产出与通货膨胀率之间的平衡关系(output-inflation trade-off).

45

This does not mean, however, that central banks do not face unemployment – inflation trade-offs as they implement monetary policy. In fact, recent research in macroeconomics has focused increasingly on an important trade – off involving output and inflation. Unlike the short-run trade-off between the level of output or unemployment and the level of the inflation rate that was a focus of earlier policy debates, the new emphasis is on the choice between the variability of output and the variability of inflation. The research on this variability trade-off suggests that attempting to keep inflation within a very narrow band may increase fluctuations in real output and employment. Conversely, attempts to smooth business cycle fluctuations more actively will lead to wider fluctuations in inflation. The nature of this trade-off, and even whether it really exists, is a subject of debate among economists.

　　Remark3：首句极成功地过渡并暗示出本段是前一段的深入,是一个有力的让步。末句指出:产出—通涨率之间的平衡关系,甚至说这种关系是否存在,仍然存在争论。

Realizing that the long-run effects of monetary policy determine average inflation, not average unemployment or the economy's real rate of growth, is critical to maintaining a successful policy. However, central banks still face trade-offs as they balance short-run inflation variability against short-run output variability, and this also needs to be recognized when evaluating the contribution of monetary policy to achieving macroeconomic goals.

　　Remark 4:文章末段末句重申观点:央行始终要面临平衡好产出和通货膨胀率之间的关系! 综合以上对各个段落的具体分析,大家可以体会出一篇成功的英文论述文章要求逻辑性强,衔接自然紧密,用词、句式结构要灵活多变。而这正是雅思作文考查的核心主旨!

　　文章来源:Carl E. Walsh (Professor of Economics, University of California, Santa Cruz) "The New Output-Inflation Trade-off", FRBSF Economic Letter, 98-04; February 6, 1998.

2.2.3　Writing Task 2 各种问题归类概括

　　People are moral beings. So any time you tell them a story, they naturally want to find out who the good guys and bad guys are. They're looking to categorize the characters. Once they find out who's right and who's wrong, they can rest. They can dismiss the script because in their mind, the issue is solved; everything will be predictable from here on out.

Alice Bass—Alice Bass, Writer

　　其实不仅是作家像 Alice 这样提倡归类分析,在英语写作中归类分析也是很有效的一种雅思学习方法。在这一节里我们将 Writing Task 2 归类分析并给出例文,这样大家可以马上体会到每种类型的文章如何布局谋篇效果最好。我们首先阐述一下总的写作思路和结构,然后进入到各类文章的具体归类分析。大家先看下面一个范文题目:

　　You should spend about 40 minutes on this task.

　　Present a written argument or case to an educated reader with no specialist knowledge of the following topic:

　　A great many countries around the world are gradually losing their cultural identity because of the prevalence of the Internet.

　　To what extent do you agree or disagree with this statement?

　　You should use your own ideas, knowledge and experience and support your arguments with examples and relevant evidence.

　　You should write at least 250 words.

写作步骤：

1.仔细审题。Instruction 部分一般都是以"Present a written argument"开始，最后要求"You should use your own ideas..."然后画出问题陈述中的关键点（key points）。

2.确保读完问题陈述的所有内容，这样才能保证下笔写作的时候不漏点。

3.快速思考（brainstorm），确定自己的观点。在草纸上快速列出一个最简单的提纲，主要是各段的主题句（topic sentences）。

4.至少要有两个支持的分论点并有逻辑顺序的组织行文谋篇。

5.文章三大部分要记牢：introductory statement，body and conclusion.

具体文章的结构还要根据问题的类型不同稍有变化。下面给大家分类讲解。

第一类：论证类（argument）

这是议论文考试非常常见的一种题型。论证类问题的特点是问你同意还是不同意或者是从多大程度上同意题目给出的陈述内容。

如：2004年4月的雅思考题：

The high sales of popular consumer goods reflect the power of the advertising but not the real need of the whole society in which they sell.

To what extent do you agree or disagree with this statement?

这里我们为大家总结出下面的万能写作结构。三部分法：

【段1】

开始段（Introduction）包含以下三点（句）。
Opening - general statement introducing the topic using different sentence structure from what is given in the question. 利用"同义转换"的手法引入主题。
Background information. 相关的背景信息。
Scope and thesis statement. 文章陈述的内容和中心主题。

* 切记：一定要给出你的中心主题，即你的观点！

【段2】

正文部分第1段——正面论证（pro-argument and justification）
Topic sentence/main point
Supporting sentence 1
Supporting sentence 2
Supporting sentence 3
正文部分第2段——正面论证（pro-argument and justification）
正文部分第3段——反驳反面观点（con-argument and justification） 这一部分要指出对立面的问题和弱点，从而强化你的论点。

48

【段3】

结论（Conclusion）
切记使用同义转换技巧重述你的主题观点

经典范文示范

Writing Task 2 Topic:

防御能力.

A government's role is only to provide defence capability and urban infrastructure（roads, water supplies, etc.）All other services（e.g. education, health, social security）should be provided by private groups or individuals in the community.

【分析】

题目要求内容 – A government's role

必须给出观点：Do I think the statement is true? Is it true in all cases and countries? Do I disagree entirely with the statement?

写作中要包括：Explain what you think a government should do. Give reasons for your opinion, with examples to show why your reasons are right. Give reasons and examples to show why other opinions are not right.

【经典范文】①

A government must provide those services which are essential to a country.

---

① 出自 Alannah 的范文。

分① These include defence capabilities and social security. Private enterprise and the profit motives should not form part of these essential services. On the other hand, some services could be provided by either government or private groups or both. Education and health care are examples of such services. A government must provide at least a basic level of education and health care so all citizens can have access to them. Private enterprise, though, could also provide services in these areas for those who wish to pay for them.

分② Urban infrastructure is another area where government and private groups or individuals can share responsibility. Governments must build and maintain a system of roads, but toll roads can be built and road maintenance carried out by private contractors. Similarly, other infrastructures, like those for water or electricity supply, can be operated by private companies. Some developed countries offer us very good examples. For example, government in the UK is responsible for constructing various roads and maintaining the motorway system, while some private companies take care of tolls.

49

尾 To sum up, there are some services such as defence and social security which must be provided by government. Other services, for example water supply or education, could be provided by both government and private enterprises. Consequently, it is not true to say that a government's role is only to provide some services while others should be provided by the private sector. In fact, both government and private groups can share in the provision of most services.

结尾重述观点,但切记用同义转换表达,不要简单重复首段或是给出的内容。

Report 第二类:解决问题型——**Problems (effect or cause)/Solutions**

下面给出两个"解决问题"型的议论文题目。

Effect & Solutions

Children are spending more time at their computers today than playing with their friends. What are the negative consequences of this over-dependence on computers and how can they be avoided?

Cause & Solutions

Overpopulation is a big concern in this century. What are the reasons for overpopulation and how can overpopulation be controlled?

解决问题型文章的万能写作模式：

【段1】

> **Introduction**
>
> The outline of problem.
>
> The scope. 范围

【段2】

> **问题1（负面影响/negative effect）—（Problem 1—cause or effect）**
> - Topic sentence
> - Supporting sentence 1
> - Supporting sentence 2
> - Supporting sentence 3

【段3】

> **问题2（负面影响/negative effect）—（Problem 2—cause or effect）**
> - Topic sentence
> - Supporting sentence 1
> - Supporting sentence 2
> - Supporting sentence 3

【段4】

> **解决方法（＊Solutions to problems 1 & 2）**
>
> ＊记住：一定要 evaluate 解决方法。

【段5】

> **结论（Conclusion）**
> - Summary of your main points.
> - View on best solution.

【经典范文】

The escalating amount of time children are spending on computers has raised questions about how the use of computer technology may be affecting their lives—from helping with their studies to causing mild forms of depression to encouraging sadistic behavior. This discussion will attempt to provide an overview of the often negative and sometimes positive effects of home computer use on children's physical, cognitive, and social development. A lot of recent news stories found on television, in the newspapers and on the Internet suggest that access to computers increases the total amount of time children spend in front of a television or computer screen at the expense of other activities, thereby increasing their chances of becoming obese. At the same time, educational research suggests that playing computer games can be an unparalleled source for building up computer literacy because it increases children's ability to read and visualize images in three-dimensional space and to track multiple images simultaneously. This further indicates that home computer use is linked to somewhat better academic performance. Many parents agree that their children will be at a disadvantage if they do not have access to computers in this highly competitive world.

51

Although there is little hard evidence to indicate that moderate computer use has a negative impact on children's friendships and family relationships, recent survey data show that increased use of the Internet may be linked to increases in loneliness and despair. Of most concern are the findings that playing sadistic computer games may increase aggressiveness and desensitize a child to suffering, and that the use of computers may distort a child's ability to distinguish real life from simulation.

I believe, therefore, that given the current trend in increased computer use throughout the world that more systematic research is needed in these areas to help parents and policymakers maximize the positive effects and to minimize the negative effects of home computers in children's lives.

第三类：比较和对比类
下面的题目是典型的比较和对比类议论文的题目。

Nowadays many universities offer courses through the Internet instead of face-to-face tuition.

How do you like these two methods of studying compare?

比较和对比型文章的万能写作模式：

Introduction
- Background.
- Scope & thesis.

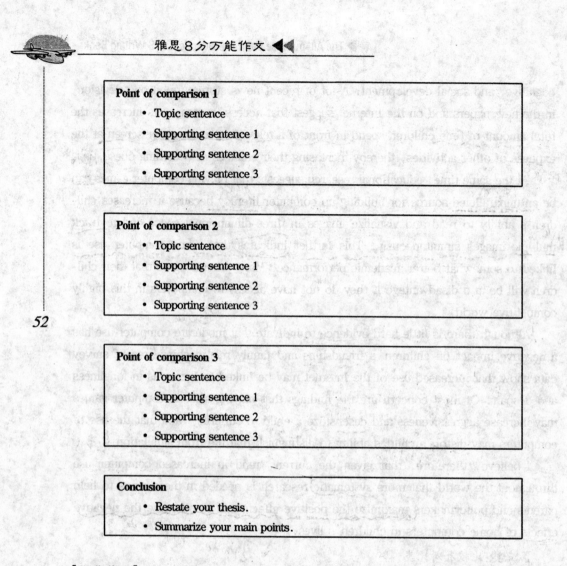

Point of comparison 1
- Topic sentence
- Supporting sentence 1
- Supporting sentence 2
- Supporting sentence 3

Point of comparison 2
- Topic sentence
- Supporting sentence 1
- Supporting sentence 2
- Supporting sentence 3

Point of comparison 3
- Topic sentence
- Supporting sentence 1
- Supporting sentence 2
- Supporting sentence 3

Conclusion
- Restate your thesis.
- Summarize your main points.

52

【经典范文】

Education, it can be argued, is on an unstoppable technology route. Knowing when to include technology in education and when not to, however, will determine how successful a particular course will be for both the teachers and students involved.

To ensure a particular university's survival in these modern times it is important that the university in question can compete and stay afloat amidst changes in information and communications technology, especially if the university in question wishes to maintain an international profile. It follows also, that if you are interested in studying a particular course you will naturally try to visit many university homepages first before making your final decision on where to study.

Ten years ago computer technology was not sophisticated enough or readily available to those students wishing to study at a distance with the full benefits shared by those students who studied on-site on university campuses. Certainly, distance courses offered by universities did exist and they were assisted by mainly print and sometimes audio and video media. Nonetheless, many people regarded these courses and the distance learning mode as inferior to face-to-face instruction in a traditional classroom environment.

Nowadays, the situation is clearly different. Those students studying online can easily meet their classmates from around the world online to build up a unique studying community through computer mediated communications. In this way, an immediate support network is established and all students are assigned to an online e-moderator who acts as a facilitator for their online discussions and individual assessment work.

Web cameras also make it possible for video conferences between small groups of students and their teachers. Limited now are the days of being one of the many faces in a lecture theatre listening to information that is only going in one direction—from teacher to students. It is also far easier now for students to evaluate their courses online.

Now, with the rapid increase in university enrollment worldwide for e-learning courses it is evident that this new mode of education is catching on. It is often cheaper than studying onsite and is a far more flexible type of education insofar as course participants can access their courses' database at any time and at any place provided they are connected to the Internet. Time is precious and the prospect of relocating and studying at a physical university is no longer practicable or necessary.

雅思考官给出如下几点考试中切记的要点：

• 关于衔接词汇和表达法：Remember to **link your ideas using linking words or phrases** within and between sentences and paragraphs.

- 关于句式、词汇多变：Also remember that you will receive a higher mark if your **use a range of structures and vocabulary**.

- 关于不要照搬题目的原话：**Don't copy from the question as this will not be assessed. Use your own words**.

- 关于时间限制：**Don't take more than 40 minutes** over this task.

- 关于字数要求：You will **lose marks** if your essay has **less than** the required number of words.

最后，在我们结束 Writing Task 2 的讲解之前，再次提醒大家回顾一下我们提到的关键点。如果你过关了。继续和作者一起进入到下一章节吧！

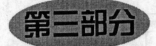

Writing Task 1
范文临摹

All human wisdom is summed up in two words: wait and hope.

人类所有的智慧可以归结为两个词——等待和希望。

——*Alexandre Dumas Pére* 大仲马

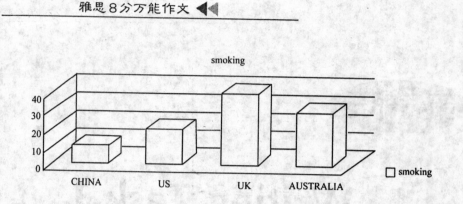

Bar Charts, like pie charts, are useful for comparing classes or groups of data. In bar charts, a class or group can have a single category of data, or they can be broken down further into multiple categories for greater depth of analysis.

—SkyMark Corporation

56

雅思写作中的第一部分是图表作文。关于图表作文的具体分项讲解已经在本书的第二部分中详细讲过,这里不再赘述,这里给大家提供了15篇与考试真题模式一样的范文,大家仔细体会文章中的用词并加以背诵,未来的考试不会脱离这些内容。最重要的是能举一反三,真正让本书成为你的8分万能作文!为方便读者,经典范文中的五星级词汇和表达均用粗体字给出,这些也是万能表达,请大家反复模仿记忆!

Writing Task 1　经典范文15篇

示范练习1

You should spend about 20 minutes on this task.

The graph below shows how the number of people receiving higher education in China has changed.

Write a report for a university lecturer describing the information in the graph below.

You should write at least 150 words.

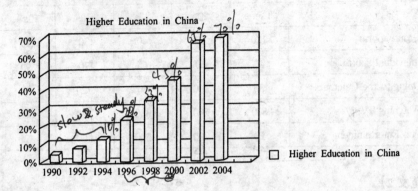

Higher Education in China

【经典范文1】

This bar graph **shows** trends in student enrollment in higher education throughout China from 1990 to the present year 2004. According to the graph, student numbers in Chinese higher education institutions have **rocketed** over the fifteen-year period. Indeed, a staggering 65% increase in the total number of students enrolled in courses for higher learning has been recorded between the years 1990 and 2004.

There was a **slow and steady** increase in Chinese tertiary student numbers from 1990 to 1994, ranging from 5% to just over 10%. This figure doubled in the next two years to reach a little over 20% in 1996. From that moment on, significant jumps in the number of Chinese students enrolled in higher education averaged at 10% between the years 1996 to 1998 and to 2000 respectively. The most noteworthy increase was recorded in the period between the years 2000 and 2002 where numbers in higher education in China rose **dramatically** from around 45% to **approximately** 65%. This appears to have started to level off in the last two years with only a slight increase in student numbers from 65% to fewer than 70% in 2004.

示范练习 2

You should spend about 20 minutes on this task.

Write a report for a university lecturer describing the information in the table below.

You should write at least 150 words.

{ the number of
the amount of

Hours of Leisure Time Spent Annually in the U.K.					
Age	Teens	20s	30s	40s	50s +
Group sports	120	70	40	30	10
Individual sports	40	60	65	70	90
Going to the Cinema	30	100	80	120	40
Watching TV	800	500	380	420	600
Pub Entertainment	20	200	300	400	120

58

【经典范文 2】

    This table **represents** the amount of time spent **annually** on different leisure activities by various age groups in the United Kingdom. The British subjects surveyed were teenagers and adults in their twenties, thirties, forties, and those aged fifty and over. The leisure activities that were the focus of this research were group sports, individual sports, going to the cinema, watching TV, and pub entertainment.

    According to the data, people in their twenties, thirties and forties enjoy more leisure time at the activities mentioned in this table. **On the other hand**, UK residents who are in their teens and those who are over the age of fifty tend to spend less time engaging in the same pastime activities. **Interestingly**, the most active age groups recorded as spending **the majority of** their free time in pub environments were in their twenties and thirties at 300 and 400 hours **respectively**. **Not surprisingly**, British adolescents are rated as the highest television viewers, spending 800 hours per annum, year which is by far the cheapest and most accessible means of entertainment listed in this table. Also discernable is a notable shift away from group sports which are enjoyed by British people in their teens and twenties toward **individual** sports which are popular among those people in their thirties, forties, fifties and over.

示范练习 3

You should spend about 20 minutes on this task.

Write a report for a university lecturer describing the information in the charts below.

You should write at least 150 words.

Water on the Earth and its uses in China, the U.S., and the U.K.

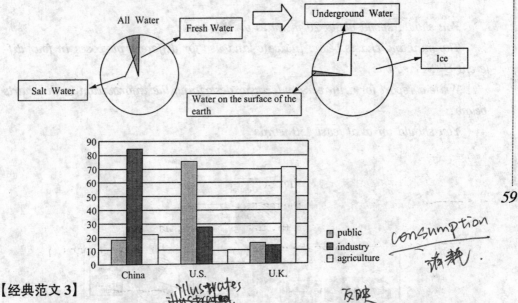

59

【经典范文 3】

The graphic information **presented** in these pie charts <u>reflects</u> the major sources of water on and under the surface of the earth. The **accompanying** bar chart **shows** how water is used in the following three countries: China, the U.S. and the U.K.

Consistent with the data in the first pie chart, the entire body of the world's water sources is **predominantly made up** of fresh water with only a small quantity of salt water making up the remainder. Nevertheless, according to the second pie chart, the bulk of the world's fresh water is actually ice, **followed by** a <u>considerable amount of</u> underground water and a <u>small</u> (**portion**) of water which is actually found running on the earth's surface.

When we study the **associated** bar chart, it is apparent that all three countries listed have quite different uses for water. A staggering 75% of all water used in the U.S. is for public consumption. China, on the other hand, <u>far outweighs</u> the other two countries in its use of water for industry with 85% being the figure recorded. Additionally, agriculture in Britain **claims** by <u>far the highest percentage of water use out</u> of the three countries listed, at 70%.

示范练习 4

You should spend about 20 minutes on this task.

The map and charts below indicate land use for different purposes in four different U.S. regions.

Write a report for a university lecturer describing the information in the charts below.

You should write at least 150 words.

60

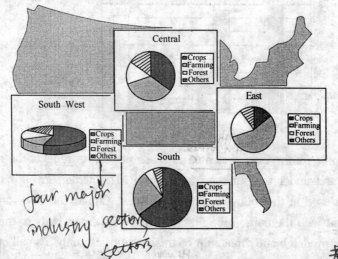

four major
industry sector
sectors

【经典范文 4】

    This map of the United States and the accompanying pie charts take into account the land use for four major industry sectors: crops, farming, forestry, and other industries, across four main U.S. regions: eastern, central, southern and southwestern areas.

    According to the graphic data, we can discern that land use for industry sectors is quite evenly spread in the central and eastern regions of the United States. In the southern and southwestern regions, however, crops followed by farming occupy far more land for these two major industry areas. Moreover, the United State's southern region has by far the lowest ratio of land use for forestry and other industries. Interestingly, America's eastern region shows a significant proportion of land use for farming which takes up over half the land required for all industries mentioned in that particular chart. If we compare the (ratios) between the four industry sectors found in the four pie charts presented here, the eastern and southern charts show the most significant differences.

示范练习 5

You should spend about 20 minutes on this task.

The diagrams below describe steel prices in the world's top five steel producing countries.

Write a report for a university lecturer describing the information in the graphs below.

You should write at least 150 words.

61

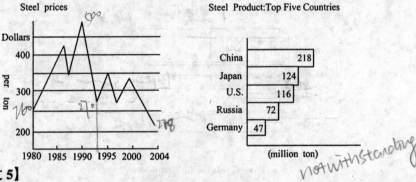

Steel prices

Steel Product:Top Five Countries

【经典范文 5】

It is clear from the line graph above that the price of steel per ton has **plummeted** somewhat over the last ten to fifteen years and that the value of steel today has **reached** an all-time low. **Notwithstanding** this trend, steel is still being produced in great amounts **throughout** the world, according to the bar graph above.

If we look closer at the bar graph we can **discern** that the biggest producers of steel are located in north East Asia, with China producing 218 million tons followed by Japan's 124 million tons. The U.S. follows closely behind Japan at 116 million tons and Russia and Germany are making somewhat lesser **contributions** in steel production at 72 million and 47 million tons **respectively**.

In 1980 the amount of dollars paid for a ton of steel was around 260 dollars, and this was **slightly** more than what would be paid in today's world in the year 2004. Remarkably, however, the price of steel **shot up to** between four and five hundred dol-

falling

lars per ton in the mid nineteen eighties and early nineteen nineties. Since then it has been a losing battle to maintain the price of steel with figures **slipping dramatically** in 1993 to 270 dollars per ton, only to make small regains in 1995 and in 2000.

示范练习 6

You should spend about 20 minutes on this task.

The charts below illustrate population trends in urban regions from four major cities around the world.

Write a report for a university lecturer describing the information in the graphs below.

You should write at least 150 words.

62

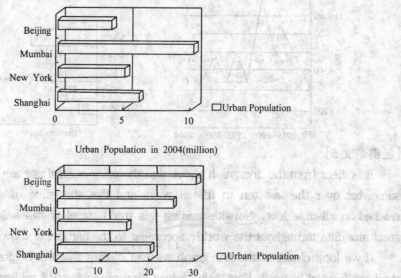

Urban Population in 1990(million)

Urban Population in 2004(million)

【经典范文 6】

The two bar graphs above **reflect** growth rates in urban populations from five major cities around the world in 1990 and in 2004. **It is evident** when **comparing** these graphs that significant increases in urban population have indeed occurred, especially in the Asian cities of Beijing, Mumbai and Shanghai. The one American city which is **represented** here has recorded gains in urban population growth; however, New

York's population growth rate is extremely moderate when put alongside those of the other three cities as reflected in these two graphs.

China's two most **prestigious** cities, Shanghai and Beijing, have **undergone** rapid growth surges in population according to the graphs. In 1990 the urban population of these cities **hovered** around the five million mark with the number of Shanghai's inhabitants slightly surpassing that of Beijing's. Nowadays, the figures are quite different with Beijing's urban population standing at a staggering twenty nine million, almost ten million more people than the number presently **residing** in Shanghai.

Mumbai, one of India's largest cities, was leading in the race for urban population in 1990 with almost ten million **inhabitants**. However, it has fallen behind the current leader, Beijing, with a population of twenty four million being recorded in 2004.

63

示范练习 7

You should spend about 20 minutes on this task.

The pie charts below reflect the percentage of fireworks accidents in Australia in 1995 and 2000.

Write a report for a university lecturer describing the information.

You should write at least 150 words.

Firework accidents in 1995

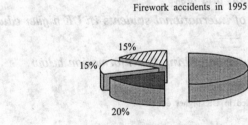
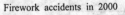

15%
15%
20%
50%

- ▨ At public displays
- ■ At family parties
- ☐ At pub celebrations
- ▨ Teens playing alone

Firework accidents in 2000

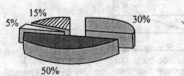
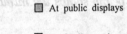
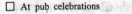
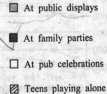

15%
5%
50%
30%

- ▨ At public displays
- ■ At family parties
- ☐ At pub celebrations
- ▨ Teens playing alone

display .

【经典范文 7】

It is clearly evident from the pie charts above that fireworks accidents in Australia were recorded as having occurred in the same places in both 1995 and in 2000; at public **displays**, family parties, pub celebrations, and in the case where teenagers were playing with fireworks **unattended**. What is notable, however, is that the ratio of accidents occurring in the different places has shifted quite dramatically in some **instances**.

By far, the **greatest proportion** of fireworks accidents were recorded as happening at public displays in 1995, at 50%. **Less than** half as many accidents **involving** fireworks, namely 20%, resulted from family parties in 1990. Furthermore, the remaining 30% of fireworks accidents were split equally between pub celebrations and where adolescents were left alone with fireworks.

Almost the **reverse** was true according to the pie chart from 2000, regarding places where fireworks accidents were most frequently recorded. Five years later almost half of the reported accidents concerning fireworks happened at family parties and only 20% occurred at public displays. A **significant drop** in figures was also recorded in 2000 for the number of fireworks accidents at pub celebrations coming in at only 5%, which was a third of those reported in 1995.

64

示范练习 8

You should spend about 20 minutes on this task.

The graph below shows the number of international students in UK higher education.

Write a report for a university lecturer describing the information below.

You should write at least 150 words.

International Students enrolled in UK higher education

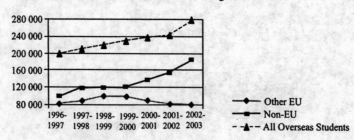

【经典范文 8】

　　This line graph shows some very **interesting trends** related to changes in international student enrollment in UK higher education. The three groups which are reflected in this graph are: other EU students, non-EU students, and all overseas students.

　　The vertical axis of this graph starts from 80,000 and goes all the way up to 280,000. From 1996/1997 to 1998/1999 the gap in student numbers studying in UK tertiary education from the three regions **remained relatively stable**. However, at around about the 1999/2000 mark things started to change somewhat. **At this point**, non-EU student numbers from Europe and all other overseas countries started to climb in numbers from 120,000 to 190,000 in 2002/2003 in the case of non-EU students and from 240,000 to 280,000 in 2002/2003 in the case of all **overseas** students. **Moreover**, at the same mid-point in time as reflected in this graph, the number of students from other EU countries enrolled in UK higher education started to decline from 100,000 to only 80,000 in 2002/2003.

示范练习 9

You should spend about 20 minutes on this task.

The table below shows the levels of stress in different occupations in the United Kingdom.

Write a report for a university lecturer describing the following information.

You should write at least 150 words.

Levels of Stress in the UK Workforce			
Rating is from zero to 10: The higher the rate the greater the pressure			
Miner	8.2	Engineer	4.2
Farmer	4.7	Dentist	7.2
Police	7.6	Doctor	6.7
Armed Forces	4.6	Teacher	6.1
Construction Worker	7.4	Postman	3.9
Journalist	7.4	Social Worker	5.9
Civil Servant	4.3	Professional Footballer	5.7
Pilot (commercial)	7.4	Bus Driver	5.3
Accountant	4.2	Stockbroker	5.4
Prison Officer	7.4	Librarian	1.9

65

【经典范文9】

Through the information that is provided in this table we can learn how different occupations rate **in terms of** stress levels on a 0-10 measurement scale: 10 being the highest level of stress.

As might be expected, jobs which are dangerous and require a lot of physical effort such as mining, policing and construction work rate highly on the stress meter; here they are 8.2, 7.6 and 7.4 **respectively**. **Somewhat surprisingly** however, according to the information in this table, the job of journalist, dentist and commercial pilot are also on the high end of the stress **scale along with** working as a prison officer. What remains truly remarkable is that being employed in the armed forces only rates at 4.6 on the same stress measurement scale.

The profession of doctor, according to the data in the table, is somewhat stressful yet it does not rate much higher than working as a teacher does. **Likewise**, being **employed** as a professional footballer is rated here as moderately stressful at 5.7 which is less than most of the other professional occupations listed in this table. Desk jobs do, however, **remain** true to their reputation and they are listed here as being relatively low on the stress gauge: civil servant 4.3, accountant 4.2, and librarian 1.9.

66

示范练习 10

You should spend about 20 minutes on this task.
The process chart below shows the stages in the writing process.
Write a report for a university lecturer describing the diagram below.
You should write at least 150 words.

Brainstorming

Rough plan/
outline

Structured
outline

Rough draft

Revising
(perhaps in
response to others'
suggestions)

Second draft

Editing/
Proofreading

Final draft

【经典范文 10】

This diagram **conveys** common stages in the writing process, from the **preliminary stage** of brainstorming ideas all the way to the highly polished final draft, which is the last stage in writing before going to press.

After the initial stage of generating ideas, a rough plan or outline usually follows in the form of a mind map. This can then be **transformed into** the next stage, which is a more tightly structured written outline. At this point, the writer will now be ready to compose a rough or first draft.

The writer will **then** arrive at the revision stage of writing, and may **seek** guidance or suggestions from other writers. After some deliberation the second draft is written in the **subsequent** stage. This in turn goes through to the final revision or proofreading stage. After everything has been checked through carefully, the piece of writing reaches the final draft stage.

67

示范练习 11

You should spend about 20 minutes on this task.

The line graph below reflects changes in employment patterns in South Korea from 1960 until 2000.

Write a report for a university lecturer describing the graph below.

You should write at least 150 words.

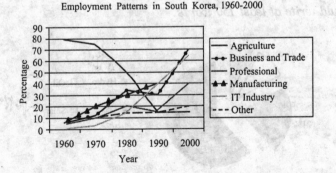

Employment Patterns in South Korea, 1960-2000

【经典范文 11】

By **briefly glancing at** this line graph, it is apparent that there were major shifts in employment patterns in South Korea between the years 1960 and 2000.

Notably, there was a massive drop in the agriculture sector from 80% in 1960 all the way down to 15% in the decade from 1990 to 2000. Conversely, all other industry sectors **presented** in the graph rose in varying degrees within the **designated** time frame presented here.

Manufacturing in South Korea made steady gains in the period of 1960 to 1990 and then shot up from 40% to 65% in the ten years following until 2000. The IT industry was **slower** to take off and made up only 15% of employment in 1980. However, there was no looking back from 1980 onwards with dramatic increases in 1990 at 40% and 65% in 2000. Indeed, the period between 1990 and 2000 shows the most marked increases in all industry sectors but agriculture and other industries. The **most significant increases** from 1990 to 2000 were in IT, which reached a monumental high of 65% and in the professional sector with 40% respectively.

示范练习 12

You should spend at least 20 minutes on this task.

The following charts represent electricity generation in New Zealand by fuel types and world energy sources.

Write a report for a university lecturer describing the information in the charts below.

You should write at least 150 words.

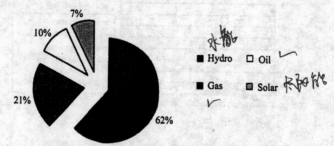

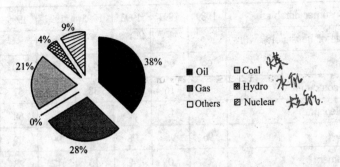

Oil Coal 煤
Gas Hydro 水很
Others Nuclear 核很.

【经典范文 12】

To begin with, the second pie chart in this task represents different energy sources in the world, and the first chart shows what percentage of different sources of energy are currently being used to generate electricity in New Zealand.

If we take a closer look at the first chart, we can discern that in 2003/2004 electricity generation in New Zealand stems from four main energy source types: hydro, gas, oil, and solar. By far, the biggest source of energy used in New Zealand to generate power is hydro dams at 62%. Compared with the second chart which shows world energy sources, hydro only makes up 28% of the total energy sources used in the world.

According to the second chart, oil is the most predominantly available energy source at 38%. Oil consumption for electricity generation in NZ, on the other hand, is kept to a minimum at only 10% of the total energy sources used.

In 2003/2004, NZ shows a reasonably high percentage of uses for solar and gas energy sources at 7% and 21% respectively. Interestingly, both hydro and solar power are renewable sources of energy, and therefore the information in these two pie charts **concludes** that NZ is consuming very little of the world's non-renewable energy sources such as oil, gas, coal, and nuclear power.

minimum 最小
maximum 最大

示范练习 13

You should spend at least 20 minutes on this task.

The table below shows the consumer durables (mobile telephones, personal computers, etc.) owned in Australia from 1989 to 2003

Write a report for a university lecturer describing the table below.

You should write at least 150 words.

69

Consumer durables	1989	1991	1993	1995	1997	1999	2001	2003
Percentage of households with:								
Television	99	99	99	99	99	99	99	99
Personal computer	5	16	24	38	48	52	80	89
Mobile telephone	3	12	32	33	35	58	69	97
Refrigerator	96	96	98	99	99	99	99	99
Digital Camera	0	0	4	10	12	28	35	42
Washing Machine	82	83	85	85	88	94	94	94
Dishwasher	7	7	10	21	32	34	35	35
Vacuum cleaner	95	96	96	96	98	98	99	99

【经典范文 13】

It is **evident** from the above table that Australian households **contained** an increasing amount of consumer durables between 1989 and 2003. All of the consumer durable items presented in this table are electronic and some have been available to the Australian public longer than others. Televisions, washing machines, and vacuum cleaners were all common household items in Australia in 1989 **according to** the information in the table. Although dishwashers were available in Australia in 1989 their sales leveled off at around 35% from 1999 to 2003.

According to the table, personal computers and mobile telephones were on the Australian market in the late 1980s and early 1990s. However, they did not rate highly as popular consumer items in Australia until the late 1990s and with the turn of the twenty-first century. The most **staggering jump** in the sale of consumer durables in Australia was with mobile telephones between the years 2001 and 2003, which **rose significantly** from 69% to 97%. Digital cameras were also a relatively new item on the Australian market in 1993-1995 and their sales picked up suddenly between 2001 and 2003 from 28% to 42%.

The information in the table **indicates** that in general Australian households had a far greater amount of consumer durables in 2003 than they did just 14 years ago in 1989.

示范练习 14

You should spend at least 20 minutes on this task.

Write a report for a university lecturer describing the information in the graph below.

You should write at least 150 words.

Crown Court Cases in the UK, 1996 – 2002

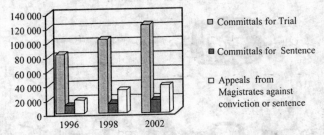

【经典范文 14】

The bar chart above shows the number of crown court cases held in the UK from 1996 to 2002. According to the information in the graph, crown court cases typically **fall into** the following three categories: committals for trial, committals for sentence, and appeals from magistrates **against** conviction or sentence.

The number of cases **recorded** for committals for trial in the UK in 1996, 1998, and 2000 **far surpassed** the number of any other crown court cases recorded. **Indeed**, there was a **steady increase** in committal for trial cases reaching just over 120,000 in 2002 which was around 20,000 up on 1998 figures and 40,000 more than was recorded in 1996.

If we look at the number of crown court cases in the UK for committals for sentence, we can see a steady growth in numbers within the six-year phase from around 10,000 to approximately 18,000. Most notably, according to the information in the graph, the growth in British crown court cases for appeals from magistrates against conviction or sentence has all but doubled in number from around 19,000 to nearly 38,000 in the same time period.

示范练习 15

You should spend at least 20 minutes on this task.

Write a report for a university lecturer describing the information in the genetic engineering process chart below.

You should write at least 150 words.

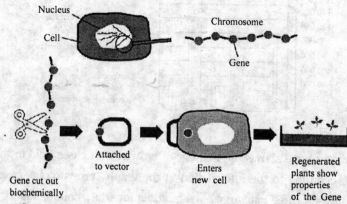

GENETIC ENGINEERING

【经典范文 15】

    This diagram shows the constituent parts of a cell and how the genetic information within a cell, which is stored in chromosomes, can be transferred to another cell to complete the process of genetic modification.

    To begin the genetic engineering process, **first of all** genes are **identified** along chromosome strands which can be found in the nucleus of a cell. **In the next stage**, particular genes are **isolated** by genetic engineers and are then biochemically cut out of their chromosomal strands. **Following this**, in the next stage, the gene is then attached to a vector, which enables the gene to enter a new cell. This combining of genetic information from one cell kind to another is the essence of the genetic engineering process.

    Finally, as in the example provided in the diagram shows; when the regenerated cells of a particular plant species are allowed to grow, the plants will show properties of the genetic information, which has been borrowed, from **another** species' cells.

第四部分

Writing Task 2
范文临摹及讲解

You have to believe in yourself. That's the secret of success.

人必须相信自己,这是成功的秘诀。

——*Charles Chaplin* 卓别林

The world can be changed by man's endeavor, and that this endeavor can lead to something new and better. No man can sever the bonds that unite him to his society simply by averting his eyes. He must ever be receptive and sensitive to the new; and have sufficient courage and skill to novel facts and to deal with them.

——*Franklin Roosevelt, American President*

美国总统罗斯福是这样说的。确实,人们通过努力可以改变世界,这种努力可以使人类达到更新的、更美好的境界。没有人仅凭闭上眼睛、不看社会现实就能割断自己与社会的联系。一个人必须保持敏感,随时准备接受新鲜事物;他必须有勇气与能力去面对新事实,解决新问题。对于我们,在模仿范文的过程中,要学会举一反三,以不变应万变,活学活用万能句子和星级词汇,真正使你的写作再上一个台阶!

说明:本部分的星级词汇以粗体字给出,而万能句子加画了横线。每篇范文都先给出"题目分析",然后是"星级词汇解析",最后给出雅思作文 7 分必备的经典句子,也就是我们所称的"万能句子解析"。首先,"题目分析"一项主要是帮助大家读懂题目,并简要地概括一下范文的布局谋篇。这一项可以有效地帮助大家背诵范文,并增强大家对范文结构模式的清晰认识。同时这一项具有帮助大家灵活记忆范文模板的功能! 其次,这里给出的星级词汇都是在雅思考试里用来提高分数的"高档次"词汇。最后,万能句子更是大家快速提高雅思作文分数的一个途径。这里的文章是雅思考官 Alannah 精心写就的;分析部分由张成思根据雅思考点和中国考生存在的实际问题用心注释的;中外教师的完美合作,这是国内的任何一本雅思备考书都无法比拟的。每篇文章都是经典中的经典,大家一定要用心体会,认真背诵。在考试里,定会下笔有神!

另外一点,如果你发现给出的星级词汇对你来说像是在读雅思阅读理解文章的难词,我们建议大家花时间背诵一下本书的姊妹篇《雅思同义词词汇必备》。这样,词汇和写作功力共同提高,最终达到阅读和写作同步提高的目标!

Writing Task 2 经典范文 30 篇

示范练习 1

Environmental hazards are often too great for particular countries or individu-

als to tackle. We have arrived at a point in time where the only way to lessen environmental problems is at an international level.

To what extent do you agree or disagree?

Environmental problems have reached such proportions that people feel international organizations must be set up to **intervene** in world affairs to resolve these problems. Whether this will resolve the problem is very **unlikely** as international organizations are just an extension of human behavior. That is, if human conflicts cannot be resolved at home, then they are unlikely to be resolved at the international level. **Nevertheless**, international organizations do attract attention to the growing problem of pollution and the destruction of the environment. However, although I **respect** the aims of the international community to resolve the issue of environmental pollution and support their cause, I do not believe it is the best or only way to protect the environment; in fact, it is only a small part of what is needed in a global **initiative**.

All world problems, whether it is environmental pollution, war, energy insufficiency, or **famine**, arise from the **abusive** behavior of all individuals. Therefore, the solution to all these problems is the need for a **collective consciousness**. What is meant by this is that each individual must be aware of the impact he or she has on the world and their unique part to play in this world. After all, if one is happy with his life, he will surely not **endeavor** to harm the environment or anyone else. His behavior will be that of a responsible individual.

What is needed, therefore, is education. Education is the key to all problems and it starts from **pregnancy** all the way to adulthood and beyond. **Furthermore**, education means that children all over the world should be allowed to go to schools with good teachers and where teaching materials and methods can be adapted to each individual. Education means raising children to be responsible individuals.

This may sound like **utopia**, but it is not: if a country has important problems in its educational system, then it should realize that it is contributing to the world's problems. These are perhaps long term solutions, but they are more realistic solutions than setting up yet another international organization.

【题目分析】

"环境问题现在非常严重了,严重到单个的国家或者是个人没法解决的程度。换言之,我们已经到了一个只有在全世界范围内才可以解决这个问题的地步。"

范文首句直接引入谈论的主题内容。"international organizations"是一种避免与

75

原题给出的"international level"重复的技巧。第一段作者用了两句话提出了观点 "Whether this will resolve the problem is very unlikely as international organizations are just an extension of human behavior. That is, if human conflicts cannot be resolved at home, then they are unlikely to be resolved at the international level."作者的观点是这个问题的解决单靠 international organizations(即 international level)是不可能的(unlikely)。"Nevertheless"引出的那句话是让步。首段末尾一句再次叙述了一下观点! 第 2 段开始具体论证。第 3 段进了一步,给出了一个可行的解决方案:education。最后一段总结。

【评分】9.观点明确,脉络清楚,层次清晰,用词多变,句式表达丰富。

【星级词汇解析】

intervene *vt.* "干预"。

76

unlikely *adj.* "不可能的"。这个小词很简单,但却常常被遗忘。其实这是一个很有威力的词,一定要记住并使用。

nevertheless *adv.* "但是"。极好的转折连词。

respect *vt.* "尊敬"。词倒不难,但是能想起用在这里很难。

initiative *n.* "主动性"。

famine *n.* "饥荒"。真正的五星级词汇。

abusive *adj.* "滥用的;破坏性的"。

collective consciousness: "集体的意识;集体的觉悟"。注意词性变化后意思的细微差别。

endeavor *n.* "努力"。

pregnancy *n.* "怀孕"。但这里指的是"一开始"之意。

furthermore *adv.* 很好的递进关系词。

|ˌjuːˈtəʊpɪə|

utopia *n.* 本意是"乌托邦",指的是"理想中的美好境界"。绝对让考官佩服你的星级词。

【万能句子解析】

(1)I do not believe it is the best or only way to protect the environment.

这是陈述作者观点的句子。大家注意这样表达的精确性。

(2)What is meant by this is that each individual must be aware of the impact he or she has on the world and their unique part to play in this world.

What is meant by this 是 what 引导的一个名词性从句作主语。整个句子是个"复合复杂"句子。

雅思中一定要注意这几句的用法。很简单,记住这句话,稍加改装就可以成为百试不爽的万能句子了。

(3)What is needed, therefore, is education.

注意这句话的逻辑关系性,用了 therefore 在中间,使文章衔接非常自然通畅。还记得我们讲过的"行文如流水,文章方通畅"的小节吗?

示范练习 2

What differentiates one country from another is becoming increasingly difficult to define in today's world. Nowadays, it is not uncommon for people to have the same consumer products and to experience the same media the world over.

To what extent do the advantages outweigh the disadvantages?

Globalization certainly has the potential to bring about great advances for humankind. On a daily basis, we are **eyewitnesses** to how borders of time and space that once separated countries and the activities **therein** appear to be **diminishing**.

In industrialized areas of the developing world we can observe a growing international trend in leisure time **pursuits**. Chinese youths wearing Nike sneakers in Shanghai hang out in Starbucks over a cup of coffee in much the same way that their American **counterparts** do in New York. In particular, younger generations the world over who can **afford** access to media technologies like cable television and the Internet often **encounter** the same media such as advertisements, films, TV channels, popular brands and so on.

However, it is not presently **guaranteed** that these advances are equally shared by all members of the global community. The truth lies somewhere closer to the fact that global market forces often have negative effects on the distribution of public goods such as social services, a clean environment, or **diverse** cultural expression.

Many argue that the costs of globalization are too high and that differences between countries and communities need to be **maintained** before we quickly and completely lose all sense of who we are, where we came from and what choices are still available to us.

Therefore, it is necessary for the global community to place greater emphasis on the impact of globalization on human welfare. In order to achieve a just and equal distribution of the benefits of economic globalization, its negative side effects need to be counteracted by reforms in government at the international, regional and local levels.

77

Only by further developing the way in which we manage our societies can we make sure that those currently not in control of globalization can make their voices heard in the political processes affecting the range of their own personal choices.

【题目分析】

题目中"*To what extent do the advantages outweigh the disadvantages?*"问的是"全球化(globalization)优点要比缺点好多少",所以作者在首段就暗示出全球化"显然会带来好处(Globalization certainly has the potential to bring about great advances for humankind.)"由于问题给出的形式很特殊,即题目本身把观点给出来了,考生要做的就是去论证这个给定的观点。从实质上讲这个题目并不是太新的形式,只是省去了大家确定观点的过程。文章开始的这句话是一句非常棒的表达观点用的"万能"句子! 首段给出观点,第2段、第3段正面论证,第4段让步分析,最后总结。

78 【评分】9

【星级词汇解析】

globalization *n*."全球化"。我们经常使用"modernization and globalization"这种"押韵"的表达方式增强效果。比如说:The speaker will illustrate how people in poverty should learn to survive and thrive as well.这里"survive and thrive"就是一个极好的示范例子!

eyewitness *n*.见证人

therein *adv*.在那里

diminishing 逐渐减少的。这个词在许多情况下可以表示"……逐渐减弱的"等意思。比如说"the effects of traditional culture are diminishing..."。

pursuit *n*.追击;追求

counterpart *n*.副本,极相似的人或物

afford *vt*.能买得起

guarantee *n*.保证　*vt*.保证。注意这个词汇的拼写!

diverse *adj*.不同的,变化多的

maintain *vt*.维持

therefore 虽"小"却实用的承上启下词汇!

welfare *n*.福利　*adj*.福利的。想过把这样的词汇用在你自己的写作里吗?

affect *vt*.影响,感动

【万能句子解析】

(1)"Many argue that the costs of globalization are...",表示许多人会说"……"

(2)"Only by further developing the way in which we manage our societies can we make sure that..."倒装句式。雅思作文其中一个要求就是考生能运用不同的句式表达,所以希望大家能记住这样稍微复杂的倒装句式,让你的作文上一个层次!

示范练习 3

Many old buildings are protected by historic trusts and international organizations such as UNESCO. However, some people think that old buildings stand in the way of progress.

How important do you think it is to protect old buildings?

Historic buildings provide a physical link to our past. This link allows us to develop a sense of orientation about our place in history. We can learn from the past, and through **safeguarding** our historic buildings, can continue to benefit from the accomplishments of our **ancestors**.

Of course, most people would be hesitant to knock down a historic building in favor of creating a new apartment **complex** or an office **block** to meet the **rising** needs of a growing population and a changing economy. This is where the question of what is "historic" and of value to a particular community comes into play. Age is a **decisive** factor for a historic resource, but it must be defined in relative terms. The definition of "old" will differ with a person's **perspective** in time and the resource being considered. A convenience store that is 25 years old might be considered historic, while a university campus might not be considered historic until it is 50 or 75 years old.

All too often, we have seen and continue to see neighborhoods being bulldozed in the name of progress. Under gentrification, housing prices rise in the previously poor neighborhoods, so that renters there either have to relocate or absorb **elevated** rental costs. What should stand in the way of progress is not only history but practicality and a thorough assessment of what is more beneficial for everyone concerned. Only when it is more costly to keep up a building or a district should town and city planners consider redevelopment as an option.

Historic buildings are an important building block in the flow of our culture through time: a child visits a historic civic building to learn more about what it means to be a native of his or her hometown; a city resident on a historic farm learns about pride and dedication in working the land. Historic buildings are studied to tell us about the use of materials and resourceful solutions in everyday living.

　　Historic buildings are **vital** for our **prospective** future. These **assets** need **protection**. We cannot afford to lose the physical materials, ideas, skills and understanding of our past.

【题目分析】

　　"许多古老的建筑应该受到法律保护,因为它们是国家的历史。而有人却认为老建筑应该都推倒,以便建设新建筑供人们使用。保留古老建筑有多重要? 历史是不是应该妨碍社会的前进呢?"文章首段末尾给出观点。第2段对反面观点加以分析。第3、4段正面论证观点,第5段总结。

【评分】9

【星级词汇解析】

80

　　protect = safeguard = protection:"保护"。

　　rising = elevated:"越来越多的"。

　　上面两组(5个粗体词)是同义转换的技巧词汇运用。第一组均为"保护"之意,只是词性不同。在文章中我们用了特殊颜色加以标记。这几个词并不难,但由于使用了同义转换,使得文章浑然增色,凸显出作者的英文功底。你也可以做得到,关键在于把这项技巧立即用到你的写作中。

ancestors *n*. 祖先,前辈

complex 除了形容词"复杂的",这里意思是名词"综合建筑楼群"

block *n*. "单元"

decisive *adj*. 决定性的

perspective *n*. "角度,层面"。使用频率很高。

vital = very important.

prospective *adj*. 预期的

【万能句子解析】

　　(1)...growing population and a changing economy:对称押韵的句式用法。

　　(2)we have seen and continue to see...:这个意思适用于太多的场合了,记住了可以普遍使用!

　　(3)We cannot afford to:在议论文结尾时除了重申观点外,如果要加一句对于反面观点的"打击",这个句式就再好不过了!

示范练习 4

In light of the technological route that education is on tod
speculation as to the role of teachers in future education. To wrat
think teachers are being replaced by computers?

Information and Communications Technology (ICT) is quickly playing an important part in teaching in schools and other educational institutions. As more and more subjects can be taught via the computer, there would seem to be less and less need for teachers to be present, as self-study and autonomous learning are encouraged with the assistance of a computer. However, computers will never replace teachers because technology is only a tool and can never replace the spiritual element of the teacher.

81

Self-study and independent learning using technology is a **means** of teaching that can be highly effective for practice drills, the study of factual knowledge, or for pure rote memorization. For instance, computers can help students solve math exercises and memorize historical facts. This type of teaching reduces the need of the presence of a teacher. **Online teaching** or video conferencing allows a teacher to teach to a greater number of students, **optimizing** costs for schools. This is already happening at the university level where many universities are offering online degrees, for example. Such teaching is profitable to universities as it optimizes costs by increasing teacher-student ratios. It would therefore seem that technology is making the teacher more and more redundant.

But a **crucial** element has to be considered with regards to ICT and teaching. Good teaching takes place when the learning is **directly associated with** our emotions. We learn best when what we are learning has a direct implication on what we believe and what we feel. The computer may communicate concrete knowledge, but only the teacher is able to communicate wisdom, to build self-confidence, and to make one think creatively, which is a more important part of learning. Therefore, no matter how **sophisticated** technology becomes, a teacher will always be needed, because only with the presence of the teacher is their true interaction.

What will happen is that technology will not replace teachers. **Instead**, teachers will no longer be able to teach students by **rote** memory or **drill** type exercises. The computer will **take care of** that. The teacher will have to stimulate the minds and bring out the **creativity** in his or her students. The teacher will have to become a better teacher, a real teacher. ICT will improve teaching, and force teachers to be better teachers; it will never replace the teacher, it will only make him or her more important.

【题目分析】

"当今教育随着技术发展的趋势,确实应该考虑一下教师在未来教育中的角色了。在多大程度上教师会被电脑所取代呢。"文章首段尾句给出观点。第2段让步,承认"技术"确实有助于教学发展。第3段马上接下来正面论证观点(computers cannot replace the teacher),第4段总结全文。

【评分】 9

【星级词汇解析】

in light of *adv*. 按照,根据
online teaching 网络教学
crucial *adj*. 关键的
sophisticated *adj*. 复杂的,久经世故的
rote *n*. 死记硬背,机械的做法
take care of 在这里表达"由……来做"

means *n*. 方式,方法
optimize *vt*. 优化
be associated with 与……相关的
instead *adv*. 相反
drill *vt*. 反复练习

【万能句子解析】

(1) As more and more subjects can be taught via the computer, there would seem to be less and less need for teachers to be present...

这种对称(more and more...less and less)的用法魅力无穷,精彩无限! 一定要记住。我们很容易造个万能句子,比如:"More and more Chinese students are studying abroad because of less and less financial burden they have nowadays!" 长我们大中国士气,灭鬼佬威风,还我们雅思高分! 我们就是富有,我们就是强大!

(2) However, computers will never replace teachers because technology is only a tool and can never replace the spiritual element of the teacher.

Good teaching takes place when the learning is directly associated with our emotions.

前一句的 spiritual element 和后句的 emotions 相呼应。同时,表示"……只是……"的句子可以用在所有对立面的事物的介绍上。

(3) The computer may communicate concrete knowledge, but only the teacher is

able to communicate wisdom, to build self-confidence, and to make one think creatively,...

(4) What will happen is that technology will not replace teachers. The computer will take care of that. The teacher will have to stimulate the minds and bring out the creativity in his or her students.

把(3)与(4)结合看。首先注意 **creatively** 与 **creativity** 的转换手法之巧妙！其次，"what will happen is that..."这是个放诸四海而皆准的句子。所以结尾段重述观点时，为了避免和首段重复，就采用这个句子！

(5)It will never replace the teacher, it will only make him or her more important. 再次体会将句式、表达活学活用的妙处。

示范练习 5   83

Should criminals be punished with lengthy jail terms or be re-educated and re-habilitated using, for instance, community service programmes, before being re-introduced to society.

Present a written case or argument to an educated non-specialist audience on the above topic.

Criminal offenders are imprisoned and released too many times. There is no real **intercession** until criminality is firmly in place and has become an all-**encompassing** lifestyle. It would appear that our sentencing policies are conflicting, often too soft for violent crimes and too **harsh** for non-violent crimes.

In addition, our public safety arrangements are too **shortsighted**. It would be better to spend more on concentrated **probation** and scientifically based rehabilitation programs now, and less on more secure prisons tomorrow. Too many people including decision-makers believe that rehabilitation programmes for **inmates** do not work, although research proves otherwise.

We also have the **tendency** to make **convicted felons** an untouchable class, isolating them from normal society and meaningful employment, making nonstop criminal activity all the more attractive.

I believe that if we were to rate prisons in the same way that we rate schools: by their success, we would establish a far more effective prison system. Achievement would be calculated by the percentage of released prisoners who are not charged with new crimes within a year, and again within two years. Yes, we would need to be in command of such factors as age, past record, and anticipated **recidivism** rates for the type of crimes each was convicted of. However, this should be fairly easy in today's computer age. This would persuade prison administrations to develop and endorse job training, anger management classes, release preparation programs, education, and other interventions known to lessen recidivism.

Another **initiative** would be to encourage those rehabilitated former offenders to become involved in teaching others. By bringing them into jails to speak to inmates and tell their own success stories, we would be able to set up a kind of adult "big brother" program where past offenders can be called on for advice or just encouragement. Is not reducing criminal recidivism worth some innovation?

84

【题目分析】

"罪犯应该长期监禁还是应该对他们进行再教育,并在他们重新进入社会之前,做一些社区服务使他们改过自新为社会所用。谈谈你的观点。"有的同学对 rehabilitate("使重新就业")这个词不熟悉,导致没有完全理解题目。在考场上如果遇到这样的题目,大家不要慌乱,其实其他的内容你一定明白,凭借前后文,就可以明白题目的内容。文章主要从"如何解决问题"这种类型文章的写法入手:首段尾句陈述存在的问题(our sentencing policies are conflicting)。第2段、第3段进一步阐述存在的问题。第4段、第5段提出作者认为可行的解决方案。

【评分】 9

【星级词汇解析】

rehabilitate v. 使(身体)康复,使恢复名誉	intercession n. 代为求情,调解
encompassing v. 包围,环绕	harsh adj. 粗糙的,苛刻的
shortsighted adj. 近视的,眼光短浅的	probation n. 试用,证明,察看
inmate n. 同住者,居民	tendency n. 趋向,倾向
convicted felon vt. 证明有罪的罪犯	recidivism n. 累犯
initiative n. 主动	

【万能句子解析】

(1) I believe that if we were to rate prisons in the same way that we rate schools...

Another initiative would be to encourage those rehabilitated former offenders to become involved in teaching others.

这两句话分别是倒数第2段和最后一段的开始句,呼应得极为巧妙:"another

initiative"意思就是说"另外一个积极的解决方案……"。另外
地用了"rate"的动词词性,表达"评价"的意思。

(2)Is not reducing criminal recidivism worth some innovatio
反问句增加号召的力度。

示范练习 6

Television is a very powerful medium of influence over large populations. There are many positive aspects to television. For example, it is an educational tool. However, many people feel that it is doing irreparable harm.

Present an argument to highlight your opinion on this matter.

Numerous educators have envisioned television's possibilities as an instructional tool and have **sought** acknowledgment throughout the industrialized world. Educational television in the developing world has also included training which directly affects the quality of life of its audience. For example, in areas where televised broadcasts are very low, audiences may gather at community centers to view programs on **hygiene**, literacy, child care and farming practices. **In this respect**, educational television equips the group with matter-of-fact information to improve living standards. Such broadcasts best **exemplify** the global aims of educational television.

However, television broadcasting **evolved** as a profit-making entity. Within this system, efforts to employ the medium for educational purposes have always struggled to stay alive, nearly besieged by the **overflow** of entertainment programs intended to attract audiences to commercials that have educated viewers in another way—to become active consumers.

Television does not have to be violent or offensive to have a negative effect. **Excessive** television viewing of any kind has obvious psychological and physiological effects on spectators. We refer to this as the "couch potato" syndrome. Several studies have recorded that even benign television content lessens our creativity and imagination, decreases physical activity, and increases **obesity**. In the case of young viewers, lowered grades, decreased ability to handle stress and conflict, and higher levels of **aggressive** behavior with **peers** have also been clearly documented.

The most studied issue that points to the **irreparable harm of television has been the impact of media violence on children.** Over a thousand academic studies have been completed, with remarkably consistent results: media violence makes our kids more hostile, less tolerant, and more frightened of the world around them. Watching violence **desensitizes** children to **genuine** acts of violence.

Despite its apparent possibilities and the early visions of pioneer broadcasters, educational television has never reached its fullest capacity as an instructional medium and the negative effects of TV viewing continue to **outweigh** the benefits.

【题目分析】

"电视是对人们影响非常大的一种媒体。电视有许多有利的方面,比如说可以作为教育的工具。但也有人认为电视带来的负面影响也极大。谈谈你的观点。"文章首段第一句是典型的"同义转换"。"instructional tool"="educational tool"。文章的结构安排是这样的:第 1 段阐述电视对教育的正面作用。第 2 段开始陈述反面现象"evolved as a profit-making entity"。第 3 段让步,说"TV does not have to be violent or offensive"。第 4 段进一步,指出电视的害处确实很大。末段给出观点"the negative effects of TV viewing continue to outweigh the benefits"。

【评分】9

【星级词汇解析】

numerous *adj*. 许多的,无数的	seek *v*. 寻找,寻求
hygiene *n*. 卫生,卫生学	in this respect 从这个角度看
exemplify *vt*. 例证,作为……例子	evolve *v*. (使)发展,(使)进展
overflow *n*. 溢出,超值 *v*. (使)泛滥	excessive *adj*. 过多的,过分的
syndrome *n*. 综合病症	obesity *n*. 肥胖,肥大
aggressive *adj*. 好斗的	peer *n*. 同辈人
irreparable *adj*. 不能挽回的	desensitize *vt*. 减少感光性,使不敏感
genuine *adj*. 真实的,真正的,诚恳的	outweigh *v*. 超过

【万能句子解析】

(1)Television does not have to be violent or offensive to have a negative effect.
显然,如果文章的主题换成 cars, computers 等等,我们都可以用这句话表示"……不一定非要有……缺点"。

(2) We refer to this as the "couch potato" **syndrome**.
我们称这种现象为"在电视机前狂吃零食"综合症。(couch potato is an expression used to describe someone who sits in front of the TV all the time eating junk food, such as potato chips.)原来"couch potato"是指一个人老坐着不动看电视。这个常用语挺有趣,指那些懒懒散散,没有动力的人(好了,下次你就可以管你的

86

同学、朋友叫"couch potato"了)。另外,refer to sth. as...是个固定搭配,"把……当作……"。

(3) The most studied issue that points to the irreparable harm of television has been the impact of media violence on children.

画线部分是很好的万能结构,表示"被研究最多的一件关于……的事情",后半句可以采用定语从句引出任何一件事物,内容依具体要求而定,这样即"万能"使用了!

示范练习 7

Outdoor recreation such as mountain climbing, camping and hiking bring us closer to nature and are ideal activities to encourage family bonding.

To what extent do you agree or disagree with this opinion?

87

Outdoor **recreation** can best be described as leisure time which involves the pleasure and use of natural resources. These days, leisure pursuits vary from popular forms of recreation such as walking, swimming, and cycling, to other less-**prevalent** activities such as nature painting, surfing, and snowboarding. According to many people the most **imperative** reasons to **recreate** are fun, fitness and family time. Clearly, many families participate in outdoor recreation as a way to bond.

While many families continue to bond over family meals at home or in front of the television, a growing number do so through outdoor activity. These dynamic families are balancing their contribution in recreational activities with work, laundry, house cleaning and homework.

Many families make use of outdoor recreation as a means to establish bonds and **transmit** key values to children. A **sizable** number of people feel that recreation strengthens the family as a unit and the children as individuals. Not only does it teach younger family members to appreciate nature but it also helps children to develop important physical skills. More often than not parents say recreation's capacity to build self-worth and personal growth and help children develop important interpersonal skills are the most important reasons to see children active.

In addition to **strengthening** family bonds, outdoor recreation can be seen as one of the foremost reasons to care for the environment. Indeed, a sizable number say the key driver for environmental protection is to conserve recreation areas and national parks.

It is generally accepted that the key to environmentally safe recreation is responsible behavior. In addition, people argue that outdoor recreation benefits the environment because it gives them a reason to care about environmental protection. It goes without saying, therefore, that if people would follow the rules in parks and recreation areas, there would be no significant effects of their land use on the environment. All in all, outdoor recreation brings us not only closer to each other but to Mother Nature herself.

【题目分析】

"户外娱乐活动如登山、野营以及徒步旅行等可以使我们更接近自然,这类活动是理想的增进家庭团结的活动。你是否同意这种观点?"这道题目需要仔细审题,有很多同学只注意了"encourage family bonding"却忽视了"bring us closer to nature"这一点。也就是说,我们在写的文章里,两点都要写。范文做得非常好。首段引入主题,并在最后一句提出"Clearly, many families participate in outdoor recreation as a way to bond."。然后第 2 段和第 3 段马上进一步阐述现实中确实如此。第 4 段用"In addition to strengthening family bonds,"很自然地过渡到"bring us closer to environment"这个层面上来。第 5 段紧接第 4 段内容进一步论证,并在本段用"all in all"结束全文。

【评分】9

【星级词汇解析】

recreation *n*. 消遣,娱乐	prevalent *adj*. 普遍的,流行的
imperative *adj*. 紧急的,必要的	recreate *v*. (使)娱乐
transmit *vt*. 传输,转送	sizable *adj*. 相当大的,大小相当的
strengthen *v*. 加强	

【万能句子解析】

(1) It is generally accepted that...

"人们一般都接受这样一种说法……"

(2) It goes without saying, ... "毋庸冗言,很明显"的意思。

(3) All in all, outdoor recreation brings us not only closer to each other but to Mother Nature herself.

记住这种总结句式,并且用了 not only...but also 连接。

示范练习 8

The younger generation is up-to-date with new techniques and advances in sci-

ence. They are often better able to make important decisions than their parents are. To what extent do you agree or disagree with this opinion?

The Net-Generation is here and whether we like it or not younger generations are in a position to be able to make significant decisions that will affect us all.

What causes this generation to be poles apart from its **predecessors** is not just its **demographic** force but that it is the first to mature surrounded by digital media. Computers can be found everywhere and digital technologies such as cameras, video games and DVDs are now commonplace. Increasingly these new media are linked by the Internet, an increasing web of networks which is attracting a million new users monthly, <u>according to popular news sources.</u> For today's **youngsters** digital technology is no more frightening than a VCR or a **vacuum** cleaner.

For the first time in history children are more at ease, clued-up and literate than their parents about an innovation of innermost importance to society. <u>I would argue that</u> it is through this use of digital media that the N-Generation will develop and **superimpose** its culture on the rest of society.

89

Already the Net-Generation is defining itself as a **reckonable** force for social transformation. **Unfortunately**, few parents are aware of what their children are doing in **cyberspace** which intensifies the traditional norms associated with the generation gap. School officials are also struggling with the reality of students often being far more intelligent on cyber-issues and new ways of learning than their teachers. **Likewise**, corporations are trying to establish what these kids will be like as employees since they are used to very different ways of working, collaborating and creating and they discard many basic assumptions of today's companies.

<u>I believe that</u> there is no single issue more imperative than understanding what the Net-Generation intends to do with its digital **expertise**. There is a lot we can find out about a whole generation, which is in the process of taking on new media, from the children who are most **adept** in their adoption of this technology.

【题目分析】

　　"年轻一代伴着日新月异的新科技长大。所以他们比父辈更加有能力作出重要的决定。你是否同意?"文章首段直接给出观点。2、3、4 段分析原因,最后一段总结并合理延伸。

【评分】9

【星级词汇解析】

predecessors *n*. 前辈，原有事物

youngsters *n*. 年轻人，少年

reckonable *adj*. 能想得到的

cyberspace *n*. 网络空间

expertise *n*. 专家的意见，专门技术

demographic *adj*. 人口统计学的

superimpose *v*. 添加，双重

unfortunately *adv*. 不幸地

likewise *adv*. 同样地，照样地

adept *adj*. 熟练的，拿手的

【万能句子解析】

(1)...according to popular news sources.

这种用法可以有力地说明你的论证是有根据的。类似的有"according to the latest report"或者"according to the latest statistics"等等。

(2)I would argue that...

(3)I believe that...

(2)和(3)都是用来表达观点时常用的句式，不要总是重复使用 "I think" 了。

示范练习9

Over the past twenty to thirty years there has been a noticeable trend away from many forms of discipline within the family. A recent survey highlighted the fact that most people feel that parents are too permissive with their children.

Present an argument to highlight your opinion on this matter.

Approximately forty years ago, there was almost complete **consensus** regarding the cultural norm which allowed parents to use corporal punishment on their children. The acceptance of **corporal punishment** was so **profoundly imbedded** in those days that there was little difference among races, regions, genders, and educational or income groups at that time.

First and foremost, I think it is important to examine why there has been a trend in recent decades away from using conventional forms of discipline in the family. A major structural change in developed and developing societies has been the shift toward a post-industrial economic system. Employment in manufacturing has declined **drastically**, as has the demand for **unskilled** manual workers. There is an increasing demand for professional, technical, and clerical workers. These are positions which, at a minimum, demand literacy and computational skills. You may ask, what has this shift in socio-economic forces got to do with changing trends in family discipline?

It has been suggested by leading researchers in the field of sociology that parents who hope or expect their child to attend university and be employed in non-manual work occupations tend to avoid using corporal punishment. Instead, what parents aim to provide their children with is anticipatory socialization for social roles in which what is needed is information and negotiation skills rather than physical strength. To the extent that these findings are correct, the norms and practices of most post-industrial societies should be moving away from the use of corporal punishment in child rearing.

Given the rising youth crime rate in recent times, however, there may be a tendency by some parents to reconsider corporal punishment. I would say that some people, and not most, believe that parents are being too permissive of their children's negative behavior. Moreover, those people who continue to favor corporal punishment are likely to perceive recent trends away from **conventional** forms of **discipline** as a threat to the family and morality. This is the dilemma that modern-day parents and law makers are faced with.

However, what is interesting to note is that it is still not a criminal offence to use corporal punishment on your children. This fact tells us exactly how far we have come away from corporal punishment as accepted practice. The choice to use or not to use corporal punishment still resides within the family.

【题目分析】

文章首段引出要分析的主题内容。第 2 段分析题目中陈述的现象为什么会出现。第 3 段引用科学研究进行进一步的剖析阐释。第 4 段转到另一方面的分析。第 5 段精炼概括全文并给出作者的观点。大家注意,这篇范文的写作形式在最新雅思作文考试中更受考官的青睐,更能得到理想的高分!

【评分】9

【星级词汇解析】

approximately *adv*. 近似地，大约   consensus *n*. 一致同意
profoundly imbedded 根深蒂固地埋在   corporal punishment 体罚
drastically *adv*. 激烈地,彻底地   unskilled *adj*. 不熟练的
conventional *adj*. 常规的, 传统的   discipline *n*. 纪律, 学科

【万能句子解析】

(1)forty years ago, there was almost complete consensus regarding the cultural norm...

化的标准,曾有非常一致的看法"。Consensus 是雅思里常见的词汇,大

牢记住并会使用。其实不仅是文化的标准,任何 topic,都可以这样说的。

st and foremost, . . .

"的表达法。

(3)It has been suggested by leading researchers in the field of sociology that, . . .
要举例论证了吗,呵呵,现把"leading researchers"拿出来亮相,看看读者信不信
服!

外国人最讲究有力的"evidence",所以这种万能的用法信手拈来,却能使"千树
万树梨花开"!

(4). . .those people who continue to favor corporal punishment. . .
"那些还青睐……的人",favor 还可以用 fancy 代换。

92

示范练习 10 厉田:
①环境退化,我们努力下代下及责任(obligation)

As a result of countries becoming more and more industrialized, pollution has become a serious problem.

Discuss some ways that can mitigate the pollution problem.

To ensure the protection of our **scenic** global village from environmental **degradation** by mass-production and mass-consumption (mostly in developed and partially in developing countries) for ourselves and for future generations, it is the obligation of every individual and people to take an active part in environmental protection.

We have often heard that there are dangerous levels of air pollution in major cities of the world all the way from Los Angeles to Seoul. Yet little has been done to solve this problem worldwide. Researchers are telling us that it will certainly cost money to clean up **overcrowded** cities, but if we do not, there will be a greater price to pay-the price of **shortening** our own life **expectancy**.

As a result of continued pollution, we can **anticipate** higher **outlays** in health care in the future, not to mention the extra costs of cleaning up our water, and protecting our food supply. Scientists are trying to inform us that in the long run, we will save money and our natural resources by doing what it takes to **wipe out** trends in pollution now.

It seems to me that it is really a matter of having a sufficiently long term vision so that the activities of societies take into account any damages to the environment. In particular, it is for those economists in governments to incorporate the costs of harming the environment. Once we do that, it will be clearer to everyone that it will pay to change the way we currently go about functioning in society.

<u>To make one final point</u>, technologies exist now, clean technologies that produce a lot less pollution. It is just a matter of cost. This is why I think it will be very important for the industrialized world to **collaborate** very closely with the developing world so that the rich countries do not just export old, **obsolete**, and dirty technologies.

【题目分析】

"随着国家的工业化程度加深,环境污染成了一个严重的问题。请谈一下哪些方法可以减轻环境污染问题。"文章首段首先指出"every individual and people"都要有义务(obligation)积极参与到保护环境中来。第 2 段指出现存的问题"little has been done"。因而第 3 段给出这些问题导致的结果"as a result of continued pollution,..."。第 4 段开始给出第一个解决方案(首句)。第 5 段给出另一个解决方法"technologies",并最后总结。

【评分】9

【星级词汇解析】

degradation

non- biodegradable
不可降解的 adj.

scenic *adj*. 布景的, 景色优美的	degradation *n*. 降级, 降格, 退化
overcrowded *adj*. 过度拥挤的	shorten *v*. 缩短
anticipate *vt*. 预期, 期望	expectancy *n*. 期待, 期望
wipe out *v*. 擦去	outlay *n*. 费用
obsolete *adj*. 荒废的	collaborate *vi*. 合作

【万能句子解析】

(1)Yet little has been done to solve this problem worldwide.

任何解决问题的文章都可以采用这个句子说明存在的问题没有被解决。

(2)Researchers are telling us that...

这又是一句用"researchers"来"吓唬"人的句子。

(3)As a result of continued pollution...

"由于……"

(4)To make one final point...

"最后一点是……",我们往往习惯于"finally",却不知道表达这个意思可以这么来说,用一次吧,这就是你的了!

示范练习 11

Many are of the opinion that the Internet is inundating our children with dangerous information. There is however no doubt that the Internet represents great advances in communication and the dissemination of information.

Discuss the pros and cons of the Internet and present your opinion on this matter.

Bearing in mind the **likely** effects of the Internet on today's users is important, because it is an issue that is discussed daily nowadays by people in both the private and public sectors. It is an everyday occurrence to come across articles in newspapers and there has been a **visible boom** in websites devoted to the trend. I would like to argue that the importance of this topic, regarding the pros and cons of the Internet, lies somewhere in the broader framework of questions raised by the Internet debate.

The Internet as the name suggests is a complex net of computers. **Conversely**, it might be more useful to think of the Internet as a network of people who make use of computers. A significant feature of the Internet is that it offers more ways to communicate than any medium in the past; **thereby** enabling users a **variety of** ways to **retrieve** information from the same computerized network system.

It is widely accepted by most that education is something that most, if not all people come into contact with at one point or another in their lives. This contact occurs typically and to the greatest degree at an early age. The principle role of schools is to educate people about their nation and the wider world, and also to help prepare them for the job market. The problem of unemployment is a commonly recognized fact. If schools are indeed doing their best to prepare young people for the job market, then their national **curriculum** needs to reflect the skills considered necessary for the most popular work sectors.

Depending on its use, the Internet may or may not contribute to the development of key skills related to critical thinking, group work, and problem solving. Over the course of time, I believe children will most likely adopt a different and possibly greater responsibility as learners when using the Internet.

As we are all aware, there is more information offered on the World Wide Web than anyone could possibly need and most of this information is very easily reached.

94

Therefore, students have to act responsibly when choosing what information to use. The risk of being distracted while using the Internet is always there; however, even if young learners do browse off every now and then, they are still using **the most hi-tech interactive tool** we have in education for today's world.

【题目分析】

"许多人认为互联网使青少年陷在了危险的信息当中。但是互联网又毫无疑问地代表了交流和传播信息的先进。讨论一下你对互联网的正面负面影响的看法。"首段最后一句提出观点(I would like to argue that),Internet 的好与坏应该在一个更宽泛的角度去分析。第 2、3、4 段具体论述,结论在第 5 段重申。

【评分】9

【星级词汇解析】

likely *adj.* 很可能的	visible boom 明显的增加
conversely *adv.* 相反地	thereby *adv.* 因此
a variety of 许多	retrieve *v.* 找回
curriculum *n.* 课程	

on the contrary 恰恰相反
By contrast

95

【万能句子解析】

(1)...because it is an issue that is discussed daily nowadays by people in both the private and public sectors...

这句话不局限用在这个题目中,任何 topic 都可以采用。

(2)I would like to argue that...

提出观点的经常性用法。

(3)It is widely accepted by most that...

当表示"大多数人认为"的时候使用。

(4)I believe children will most likely adopt a different and possibly greater responsibility as learners when using the Internet.

用其他主题名词替换 "children"和"Internet"两个词之后,这个句子就成了一个非常迷人的万能句了。

(5)As we are all aware...

表示"大多数人都注意到",和(3)句功能类似。

示范练习 12

Salaries paid to employees are an accurate reflection of their value to society.

互眼 体现

What is your opinion?

In approaching this task, consider in particular salaries paid to nurses, doctors, sports-persons, movie stars, teachers and farmers.

Equal pay for equal work has long been an issue debated mainly in industrialized nations around the world. People argue that **varying pay scales** for workers in different employment sectors are not a true reflection of their work's value to society. So, why is it that nurses who work around the clock in hospitals the world over earn **staggeringly** less than doctors who put in much the same hours? Again, why is it that movie stars and professional sports players like David Beckham earn more money than anyone else **whereas** those in farming who are essentially feeding the world earn less than most?

96

Reasons why the wage gap exists could **be accountable to** differences in education, work experience or time in the labor force. Nonetheless, some argue that the wage gap **is attributable to** discrimination. It is quite evident that certain low-paid jobs in most societies are reserved for women, people of color, and those with limited education. One example is that nursing is primarily carried out by women and when we compare the salaries received by nurses with those of doctors who are primarily men, we are made aware that nursing is among the lowest-paid occupations in the developing and developed worlds.

However, many researchers maintain that women's average wages are lower not due to any discrimination that may exist in the world but because women choose to work part-time or in lower-paying jobs that present more **flexibility**. Teaching, for example, has always been considered to be a more flexible profession allowing women to work and have time off for raising children because of the ample vacations that come with the job.

Advocates for pay equity do not always applaud the choices that some people make and they do not want people to have to face the consequences of those choices. As far as I can see, the real issue seems to lie with the choices an individual is presented with when he or she ventures into the world of work. More importantly, what choices are available when one wants to change his or her profession later on in life?

As most of us would agree, it is often very difficult to break the poverty cycle when all that is on offer are the same jobs that were done by our parents and close neighbors before us. It remains therefore, that through education and a constant re-evaluation of the types of work we do that we will be able to find the trick to balance any **disparities** in pay.

【题目分析】

"工资是个人社会价值的准确体现。你的观点是什么？在完成这项写作任务的过程中,尤其要讨论一下护士、医生、运动员、影星、教师、还有农民的工资收入情况。"这个题目同学们普遍感到不太好写。但是范文却脉络清楚、层次清晰地娓娓道来,首段自然引入主题,并巧妙地将题目中的信息引出来,提出问题。第2段分析解释wage gap 的原因,第一句提出有些原因(differences in education, work experience or time in the labor force)来解释这个 wage gap。然后紧接着引出有些人认为的反面观点(some argue...discrimination)及例子。第3段,用研究专家的话反驳第2段那些人的说法。最后两段深入指出作者的观点和解决办法。本文例子紧贴原文题目中内容,将道理讲得十分让人信服。本文充满了值得记忆的万能表达,请大家参考下面的解析。

97

【评分】9

【星级词汇解析】

varying pay scales 不同的薪酬标准

staggeringly *adv*. 让人吃惊地

whereas *adv*. 然而,可是

be accountable to 对……负有责任的

is attributable to 归因于……

flexibility *n*. 灵活性

disparity *n*. 不同

【万能句子解析】

强烈推荐大家背诵第一段全文

(1)Equal pay for equal work has long been an issue debated mainly in industrialized nations around the world.

大家看"...has long been an issue debated mainly in...around the world",空处换上不同的主体名词,就是万能的说法了。

(2)It is quite evident that certain low-paid jobs in most societies are reserved for women, people of color, and those with limited education.

"很明显,……"后半句排比的威力,随处可用,真正万能!

(3)One example is that...

举例子时使用。

(4)...many researchers maintain that...

记住这样的用法,这样的句子使人信服。

(5)**Advocates** for pay equity do not always applaud the choices that some people make and they do not want people to have to face the consequences of those choices.

"倡导工资平等的人并不总是赞同……"applaud(赞同)使表达丰富多彩。

(6)As far as I can see...

"就我来说……"

(7)As most of us would agree...

"我们大多数人都认为……"

(8)It remains therefore, that through education and a constant re-evaluation of the types of work we do that we will be able to find the trick to balance any disparities in pay.

"因而……"的表达用法。

98

示范练习 13

Although there is no longer an immediate threat of nuclear war, peace seems as elusive as ever. In order to address this problem, the United Nations should be given a stronger role in global affairs in order to bring about world peace.

To what extent do you agree or disagree with this opinion?

The idea of world peace is arguably a recent notion in the history of mankind. Even today, with the war against terrorism, many consider the war in Iraq as inevitable and peace as only a **hazy and intangible utopian dream**. As we witnessed in the twentieth century, the first significant anti-war movements in the western world sprang up between the two world wars that is in the nineteen twenties and thirties. This was a very significant time in modern history as it **gave rise to** what was then called the League of Nations which was then the brain child of today's United Nations.

Most would agree that the United Nation's role is to prevent conflicts so that we can all live in a peaceful world that is free from terror. In this sense, I believe that the United Nations should be given a stronger role in global affairs to ensure that conflict is prevented in all corners of the world by one united governing body. **Conversely**, conflict resolution should not be left up to individual countries who take it upon themselves to ensure "peace" through invasions: America's occupation of Iraq being one such example.

The UN was established to deal with anything that could be at the source of conflicts. Weapons and warfare have regrettably become ever more deadly since the United Nations was set up. Furthermore, despite there being greater wealth in the world nowadays, its allocation **is far from** equal. Unfortunately, the difference between **the haves and the have-nots** in this world is **visible** in all places and in all countries, and is increasing. The breakout of contemporary conflicts is often related to the control of natural resources. Illiteracy also contributes to the birth of new conflicts.

The United Nations is supposed to be there to **guarantee** that fundamental human rights and freedoms are valued, <u>irrespective of where someone comes from, what they believe in or what gender they are.</u>

I believe that we should give the United Nations an even stronger role in global affairs, <u>considering the fact that there are many types of conflicts, with diverse origins and various consequences that will in time affect us all.</u>

99

【题目分析】

"尽管现在没有了立即就会发生大的核战争的危险,但是和平还是像以往一样捉摸不定。为了处理好这个问题,联合国应该扮演更强大的角色,以带来世界和平。从多大程度上你同意或者不同意这种看法。"首段引出主题,但并没有直述观点。第 2 段开始给出观点(I believe that the United Nations should be given a stronger role in...)。第 3、4 段深入阐述原因。末段总结,重申观点!

【评分】9

【星级词汇解析】

hazy and intangible utopian dream 朦胧模糊的乌托邦式的梦想

gave rise to 引起,造成

conversely *adv.* 相反   On the contrary

be far from 远不是……

the haves and the have-nots 财富的拥有者和没有财富的人(富人和穷人)

visible *adj.* 可见的   ~~available~~ 可用的.   available.   visible   available

guarantee *vt.* 保证

【万能句子解析】

(1)The idea of world peace is arguably a recent notion in the history of mankind. "The idea of..."是个万能用法。

(2)Most would agree that... 再次复习一下这个常用表达。

(3) I believe that the United Nations should be given a stronger role in global affairs to ensure that conflict is prevented in all corners of the world by one united governing body.

提出观点的句子。

(4) ...America's occupation of Iraq being one such example

举例子的说法,不落俗套(通常用"for example")。

(5) ...irrespective of where someone comes from, what they believe in or what gender they are.

万能的排比句式!

(6) ...considering the fact that there are many types of conflicts, with diverse origins and various consequences that will in time affect us all.

"考虑到……"

示范练习 14

Spending money on scientific research should only be approved when there are economic benefits resulting from the research.

Do you agree or disagree with this opinion?

A **primary** challenge for developing and post-industrial societies is not only to **garner** enough funding for scientific research but to go further in their spending for development if they want to secure positions as truly knowledge-based economies. <u>An appreciation for investing in scientific research has matured steadily in recent decades.</u> Having said this however, most would agree that it is not easy to **gauge** the direct social and economic benefits resulting from scientific research. Many of the features of our modern world are the direct results of scientific research. Computers are but one area that receives a **staggering amount** of investment as countries compete with one another for stakes in this **lucrative** market. Medical research, **likewise**, is well worth the investment that is made for finding new ways to ensure the well-being of those fortunate enough to be able to receive treatment. These are but a few obvious examples.

<u>However, what is almost certain is</u> that in many cases the time from scientific discovery to the commercialization of research results may often be long. However, there are many instances of **breakthroughs** in research that provide additional support

for the popular principle that public investment in basic science generates continued economic and social benefits.

The evidence presented in research journals available to the public confirms that government-funded research is a vital source of investment for increasing a society's knowledge and skills. When governments invest in scientific research their funding in turn **expands** the technological opportunities available to companies who wish to develop new products and processes. Such spending on scientific research also supports the education of students who **in turn** transfer their competencies in science and technology into the private commercial sector.

Due to the widespread understanding that the development of economically viable research projects is often a **lengthy** and **time-consuming** process it is natural that some people would be opposed to the idea of further government money being spent on scientific research. However, I believe the rewards from research and development are well worth waiting for in this ever changing world of ours.

【题目分析】

"只有能带来经济回报的科研项目才应该被批准。你是否同意?"首段暗示出作者的观点。但明确的观点在最后一段末尾句给出(I believe the rewards from...)。第2段、第3段分述理由,第4段总结陈词。

【评分】9

【星级词汇解析】

primary *adj*. 最主要的

gauge *vt*. 衡量,测量,考虑

lucrative *adj*. 有利可图的;赚钱的

breakthrough *n*. 突破

in turn 接着,从而

time-consuming *adj*. 耗时的

garner *vt*. 存贮

staggering amount 让人吃惊的数量

likewise *adv*. 同样道理

expand *vt*. 张开,膨胀

lengthy *adj*. 冗长的

【万能句子解析】

(1)An appreciation for investing in scientific research has matured steadily in recent decades.

"对于在科研方面的投资的正确评价近年来逐渐成熟起来了。"appreciation用在这个句式中使表达到位,准确!

(2)However, what is almost certain is...

表示强烈的事实。

(3) The evidence presented in research journals available to the public confirms that...

这种表示用法常用在举例论证中。

(4) ...some people would be opposed to the idea of...

提出反面观点的一种万能句式。

示范练习 15

Since reading is important for a good education, we should encourage our children to read extensively. However, as there is an abundance of undesirable reading matter, there should be heavy censorship to restrict access to it.

102   *What is your opinion?*

Many would agree that reading extensively is good for young people but some would argue that the consequences of reading too widely may be far from **constructive** to the often impressionable minds of youngsters in their formative years.

Censorship that is carried out for the benefit of children and teenagers is often based on the **supposition** that they have to be sheltered from "indecent" material that might damage their development in some way—whether in art performances, in books, or on a website. One may ask, however, where this assumption comes from, and to what extent is it true? In this essay, I will attempt to present both sides of this argument in order to establish my position on this issue of censorship and young people.

First and foremost, there are many people out there who **champion** the freedom to read widely which stems from a belief in the freedom of expression. They argue that this is part of the democratic process. **Nonetheless**, that freedom has been under constant attack by private groups and public authorities who are trying to remove certain books and journals from sale, to bar particular books from public schools, to silence and censor newspapers and magazines, and to basically restrict all "**contentious**" materials which may land in the laps of the general public. As far as I can see, however, censorship of reading materials leads to the repression of creative thought.

Furthermore, in recent times we have witnessed an increasing trend in children's literature that is more realistic to life, with subject matter that takes into account many **aspects** of the world around us. For example, sex and homosexuality are being presented in a lot of young people's literature in order to promote greater understanding and tolerance. Divorce and separation are also being dealt with in some children's literature as is **child abuse**, drugs and violence, etc. However, it is these realistic books that have people (mostly parents) **outraged**.

The final point that I would like to make is that the freedom to read extensively should be promoted but where children are involved, control should be exercised by access to materials and not through censorship.

【题目分析】

"因为看书对教育很重要,所以我们应该鼓励青少年广泛阅读。但是,由于存在许多内容不好的阅读材料,所以应该施行严格的管制措施。你的观点是什么?"首段引入主题但没有直述观点。第2段末句提出这篇文章的内容。第3段、第4段分别论述,最后一段结束全文的论述!

【评分】9

【星级词汇解析】

undesirable reading matter = "indecent" material 不好(不健康)的内容

constructive *adj*. 建设性的 　supposition *n*. 假定,设想

sheltered *adj*. 受保护的 　champion *vt*. 支持

nonetheless *adv*. 然而 　contentious *adj*. 有争议的 = debatable 加单议论

aspect *n*. 方面 　child abuse 虐待儿童

outraged *adj*. 狂怒 　repress 压制、抑制

【万能句子解析】

(1)Many would agree that... but some would argue that...

复习一下这个句式!

(2)In this essay, I will attempt to present both sides of this argument in order to establish my position on this issue of censorship and young people.

这种写法在分析两面的问题时可以采用。

(3)...which may land in the laps of the general public

"可能涉及到普通大众。"

(4)Furthermore, in recent times we have witnessed an increasing trend in...

"并且,最近我们已经看到了一个……的增长势头"。

(5)The final point that I would like to make is that...

用在提出最后一点观点的时候。

示范练习 16

Although many benefits may result from space exploration, the costs involved are enormous. There is some debate as to whether this money could be more wisely spent to provide for the basic needs of mankind such as food, clean water, contraception etc. For this reason space exploration should be restricted.

What is your opinion?

One giant step forward for mankind: these were the words of American astronaut, Neil Armstrong, the first man to land on the moon.

Space exploration is considered by most developed countries and those aspiring to compete in the race for development as the last **frontier** known to mankind. However, there are many people who belong to nations which have space programs who question the **expenditure** involved in continued space exploration when it is apparent that money is needed to deal with many of the world's existing problems, for example, **pandemic** situations like AIDS and poverty that are always on the increase.

A trip to the moon was an incredible success in 1969; however we have plainly taken a step backwards in the last 30 years or so. The dreams of travel to outer lying planets like Mars and Pluto remain as distant as ever, not forgetting the dream of interstellar voyages and exploring new solar systems. A big part of the problem is that our current technology is simply unable to realize these dreams. Even our best chemical rockets would take somewhere between one and two years to reach the closer planets and this is largely due to the fact that before reaching the desired destinations rocket fuel is likely to run out.

The amount of money required to fuel space exploration programs of such large proportions **begs the question** of just how feasible all this spending is. It is clearly **prohibitively** high and a key objective for the years ahead will be to lower the cost to a fraction of today's value. In the meantime however, we need to realistically face the problems existing on our earth which are far more pressing and far more concerned with true development.

Making dreams come true on this planet, of a better world for everyone to live in, is surely more achievable for mankind than reaching outer lying **galaxies** which are light years beyond our existing capabilities.

【题目分析】

　　"尽管太空探索可以带来许多好处,但投入的成本也是巨大的。人们就这些钱是应该用在太空探索上还是应该更明智一些花在人们的基本需求方面的问题展开讨论,比如食物、纯净的水、避孕措施等,就这点原因考虑,太空探索应该有所限制。你的观点如何?"本文的基本观点是反对投入大量的钱财在太空探索上面。首段引入主题,第2段和第3段分别论述为什么反对这种做法。全文最后一句强化了观点! 如果大家发现比较难理解本文,看了这个分析就清楚了。更多的问题可能是出在词汇量不足上面,所以加油背单词吧!

【评分】9

【星级词汇解析】

　　contraception = pandemic situations like AIDS voyage 首段的这个表达呼应 topic 中的内容。

　　frontier n. 前沿

　　expenditure n. 花销

　　beg the question 引发这样一个问题……

　　prohibitively adv. 禁止地

　　galaxy n. 银河系,星系

【万能句子解析】

　　(1)...was an incredible success...

　　"巨大的成功"

　　(2)...remain as distant as ever...

　　"和以前一样远"

　　(3)...realize these dreams...

　　"实现梦想"的正确说法。

　　(4)In the meantime however...

　　实用的承上启下的表达!

示范练习 17

　　Some people think that co-educational schooling is good for students while others hold that single sex education is better than co-educational schooling.

　　What is your opinion?

　　In today's modern world women find themselves in every possible position in society and are no longer relegated to separate spheres from men. <u>Likewise, it is no longer required that</u> women go to separate schools from men, <u>nor is it</u> expected that women will learn different skills from their <u>male counterparts</u>.

Nowadays, young women can still to some extent choose whether or not to attend a single-sex school, although that choice is slowly disappearing with the rise in popularity of co-educational schools. <u>I hope to explore the two sides of this phenomenon while discussing the trends in single-sex education in my response to this question.</u>

The argument is **multi-faceted** with some single sex school **advocates** arguing that separate education for girls can play a vital role in a young woman's development as she learns to **assert** herself in a more comfortable environment. Others in favor of co-ed schools argue that a separate education cannot be equal and is in reality **detrimental** to young women in that they are deprived of opportunities to assert themselves around men.

<u>Now with our entry into the twenty-first century</u>, women are experiencing more and more equal opportunities with men, although they are still far from their **ultimate goal** of **egalitarianism**. <u>It remains true that</u> many learning environments are often male-centered and to a great extent the working-world is still male-oriented.

With each new year, we are seeing more women apply to institutions of higher education and there are now as many, if not more women in **tertiary** education. Having said this, however, women still occupy far fewer positions as presidents of leading companies and they represent only a small number of those politicians in governments the world over.

<u>I believe that</u> the advancement of coeducational institutions was and is important to the future equality of women but so is the **survival** of **contemporary** all-female learning institutions.

【题目分析】

　　"有人认为男女同校教育好,而也有人认为男女分开教育的方式好。谈一下你的观点。"本文又是一篇从两方面进行分析的文章。首段引入主题。第 3、4、5 段分别分析,第 6 段总结(I believe that...)。

【评分】9

【星级词汇解析】

multi-faceted *adj*. 多层面的　　　　　　　advocate *n*. 倡导者

assert *vt*. 认为，主张

ultimate goal 最终目标

tertiary *adj*./*n*. 第三的；中专的

contemporary *adj*./*n*. 同时代的(人)

detrimental *adj*. 有害的

egalitarianism *n*. 平等主义

survival *n*. 幸存

【万能句子解析】

(1)Likewise, it is no longer required that...nor is it...

"同样道理，……同时"这是个很值得一背的倒装句式！

(2)male counterparts

意思就是"男同胞们，男性同志们"。

(3)I hope to explore the two sides of this phenomenon while discussing the trends in single-sex education in my response to this question.

"我希望能从两个方面去分析一下这个现象，……" explore 就是 "touch upon"

(谈及，分析)的意思。

(4)Others in favor of...

"还有人喜欢……"。

(5)Now with our entry into the twenty-first century...

大家很喜欢用又经常用错的一个句子："随着我们进入了21世纪……"。

(6)It remains true that...

"事实是……"。

(7)I believe that...

表达观点的"老一套"用法。

示范练习 18

Forests are the lungs of the earth. Their destruction will accelerate extinction of animals and ultimately mankind. For this reason, logging in the world's rainforests should be phased out over the next decade.

To what extent do you agree or disagree with this opinion?

The world's forests sample the best scenery and incredible natural diversity available on earth. They provide homes for **indigenous** wildlife, special historic sites and places of cultural interest. Many of the world's forests have been developed for tourism and public recreation. The governments of the world therefore have the responsibility to decide how best to manage international logging industries and forests in order to protect their special value to animals' and **ultimately** to mankind's **survival**.

One of the biggest problems facing native forests such as the Amazonian rainforests is illegal logging. The first and most obvious problem associated with the illegal felling of native forests is that it denies a livelihood to many poor people living in forest areas. This in turn robs poor governments of billions of dollars as the revenue created around the sale of native trees is sucked out of the local economy into the bank accounts of those few who are involved in such illegal operations.

A further problem is the environmental degradation that we are witnessing in forested areas of the developing world which are now being stripped bare of trees without any replanting schemes in place. As anyone who knows anything about the laws of nature will agree, forests like any living species must be adequately stocked with healthy tree **saplings**, or planted with replacement native **seedlings**. Moreover, forest operators must ensure that young trees are well established and are able to grow freely following **reforestation** procedures. Only if such measures are carried out can we allow logging to continue into future decades.

The final point that I would like to raise is that wide-scale illegal logging **provokes and sustains** conflicts in many regions of the world. As much of the logging occurring in developing countries is a consequence of poor governance, at local, national and international levels, governments need to band together to ensure this does not continue to **denude** our planet. In order to **combat** illegal logging at an international level we must ensure that trade in **timber species** is conducted in agreement with international trade laws in **endangered species**. Only through applying stricter measures in the trade of forests should we be able to protect species that all our lives depend on.

【题目分析】

"森林是地球的呼吸器。森林被破坏将会加速动物的灭绝并最终导致人类的灭亡。因此,应该逐渐停止热带雨林地区的伐木。从多大程度上你同意或者不同意这种观点。"作者的观点是强烈反对无管制的 logging,作者认为政府应该好好管理。所以首段即提出了观点。第 2 段分析 illegal logging 的危害。第 3 段进一步阐述 logging 导致了 degradatoin (第一句话)。最后一段作者提出了 final point 并再次指出政府应该更加有力地管理好 logging 问题! 文章的布局是分别在第 2,3,和 4 段首句用了"One of the biggest problems...","A further problem is...",和"The final point that I would like to raise is that..."三句衔接紧密的话使得全文如行文流水,论述得无懈可击！同学们一定要好好学习和效仿这种写作手法。

【评分】9

【星级词汇解析】

(这里有许多大家在写"环境"或者"树木、树苗"相关的文章可以用到的星级词汇！)

indigenous *adj*. 本土的	ultimately *adv*. 最终
sapling *n*. 树苗，小树	seedlings *n*. 秧苗，树苗
reforestation *n*. 重新造林	provoke *vt*. 激起，驱使
sustain *vt*. 支撑，维持	denude *vt*. 使裸露，剥下
combat *v*. 战斗，抗击	timber species 木材种类
endangered species 濒危物种	

【万能句子解析】

(1)The first and most obvious problem associated with...

在引出任何事物缺点或者毛病的时候，这句话就是强有力的万能句子。

(2)A further problem is...

表示递进关系，"另一个毛病或者问题"，使文章"超级"通畅。

(3)As anyone who knows anything about...

指出"大部分人都知道……"的句子。

(4)The final point that I would like to raise is that...

复习一下这个引出最后一个分论点的说法。

(5)provokes and sustains

"引起(话题、事情、观点等)并使之……持续"。

(6)...at local, national and international levels

掌握排比句子的用法,体会它的威力！

示范练习 19

Aquariums and wildlife sanctuaries are seen as sources of education and entertainment for families. They are also essential to conduct life-saving research. However, there is opposition to confining animals in this way.

Discuss some of the arguments for and against the maintenance of zoos and present your opinion.

The confinement of animals and marine life has always generated mixed feelings

from the general public including those who consider themselves to be **staunch** environmentalists. In this essay, I will try to reflect the positions of those who support the continuation of wildlife sanctuaries and aquariums alongside those who would like to see such institutions removed from society.

As a child, I remember visiting the local aquarium quite frequently with my family to enjoy **dolphin** and **seal** shows which were truly entertaining. In retrospect, however, I cannot **recall** the aquarium staff ever trying to teach the spectators how to protect marine life. That type of thinking was not so popular back then but things have changed in recent decades with the **advent** of environmental activist groups, such as Greenpeace and eco-friendly zoos and aquariums which have been designed to simulate natural habitats for those animals living in confinement. Needless to say, it is difficult to generalize about zoos and aquariums because to this day, places which are little more than prisons for animals still exist.

Recently, I read the 2002 Booker Award winning novel, Life of Pi, by Yann Martel which enabled me to understand this complex debate over the role of zoos and aquariums at a deeper level. In his book, Martel disclaims the widely held belief that animals living in captivity have a shorter life expectancy than those living in the wild. Instead, the main protagonist in his novel who is a zoologist, claims that the opposite is true and that in fact animals have a higher chance at survival when taken into captivity. This is largely due to the fact that natural habitats are **diminishing** because of man's **ongoing expansion** into what were once un-peopled environments.

Experts in the field of animal and marine research are currently making it possible for mankind to conserve many species that are currently at risk in their natural habitats due to rising environmental **hazards** such as illegal **poaching**, water pollution and deforestation. Perhaps we should look on zoos and aquariums as a temporary solution until a time when man can see to the conservation of the world's ever decreasing natural habitats and the wildlife that should rightfully inhabit them.

【题目分析】

"水族馆和野生动物避难所被视为家庭教育和娱乐的场所。这些地方也是进行救生研究的场所。但也有人反对以这些方式限制野生动物。就支持和反对保留动物园这些场所的论调进行讨论,并阐述你的观点。"这个题目无疑又是一道广大考生感到比较难的题目。范文首段引入主题,然后最后一句阐述出文章涵盖的内容,观点在最后一段给出。第2段从作者小时候的经验写起,末句用了"places which are little more than prisons for animals still exist"暗示过去水族馆等地方并没有什么好处。第3段引用作者自己读过的一本书为例,指出关起动物也有好处。最后4段总结,观点是,在环境恶化的情况下,动物园是一个暂时的解决方法。请背诵这样的模式,因为这类文章考生不太容易自己写出较深的论述。

【评分】9

【星级词汇解析】

confinement *n*. (被)限制	staunch *adj*. 坚定的
dolphin *n*. 海豚	seal *n*. 海豹
recall *vt*. 回忆	advent *n*. 出现,到来
diminishing *adj*. 逐渐缩小的	ongoing expansion 正在进行的扩张
hazard *n*. 危险	poaching *n*. 偷猎行为

【万能句子解析】

(1) I will try to reflect the positions of those who support the continuation of wildlife sanctuaries and aquariums alongside those who would like to see such institutions removed from society.

"我会对两方面观点都给予分析:那些支持野生动物避难所、水族馆之类场所存在的人,和那些要这些场所从社会中消失的人。"这是个很"复杂"的句子,但稍微花一点点时间,背住了,用在那些对两面观点都要求分析的文章里,定能"大得分"!

(2) As a child, I remember visiting…

这是用自己亲身例子进行论证的常用句子。

(3) Needless to say, it is difficult to generalize about…

"毋庸置疑、不用多说"的意思。

(4) Recently, I read…

举例论证常用句式。

(5) complex debate

其实雅思作文大部分都是比较"复杂的争论",不是吗? 所以这种表达可以放在任何文章当中。

示范练习 20

Although education in many developing countries is not compulsory, an effort should be made to ensure that all children between the age of 5 and 15 years attend some form of schooling.

To what extent do you agree or disagree with this opinion?

Schooling is the type of learning that occurs within recognized educational institutions and networks. This is an important distinction **insofar** as the skills one acquires in schools and colleges are recognized by society. This **validation** of one's learning **enhances** one's chances of moving upward through the ranks of society to achieve a greater standard of living. For this reason alone, an effort to educate children from developing countries must be made at all costs.

In order to satisfactorily answer this assigned question, I believe it is important to define what the flip side of not having an education means for children from developing countries between the age of 5 and 15 years. The real danger that exists here is the trap of young uneducated people falling into what is categorically referred to in the developing world as child labor. There is a clear link between child labor and poverty which I would like to bring to my readers' attention.

In many developing countries, parents, whose families exist on the poverty line, are often faced with having no food to provide their family with, so they force their children to do heavy work to ensure their family's survival. It would seem that poverty is the principal cause of child labor. **Nonetheless**, child labor continues to feed the poverty cycle. Therefore, what is required of this situation is a break in the **vicious circle** between child labor and **poverty**. This can only be achieved through an increased emphasis on education. The answer rests with education programs that occur **in conjunction with** children's work. **Abolishing** extreme forms of abusive child labor is obviously the first measure that should be taken as this type of work hinders children's health and their ability to work in the future. However, it would appear too early to make full-time education compulsory in cases where children still have to earn a living to survive.

What is important to remember is that the **extensive** use of child labor in developing countries slows down economic growth and social development. Moreover, a population that lacks sufficient skills and education **perpetuates** poverty and reduces overall progress.

【题目分析】

"尽管教育在许多发展中国家不是强制性的,但应该努力确保 5 到 15 岁的孩子接受一定形式的学校教育。在多大程度上你同意这种说法?"首段末句给出观点"an

effort to educate children from developing countries must be made at all costs."第 2
段分析没有教育的负面影响。第 3 段分析造成没有教育的原因。第 4 段给出解决方案。最后提醒人们关注这个问题,使文章得到升华。

【评分】9

【星级词汇解析】

insofar *adv*. 在……的范围 validation *n*. 确认

enhance *vt*. 增强 nonetheles *adv*. 但是

vicious circle 恶性循环 poverty *n*. 贫穷

abolish *vt*. 废弃 in conjunction with 和……一起

perpetuate *vt*. 使永存,使不朽 extensive *adj*. 广泛的

【万能句子解析】

(1)For this reason alone, an effort to...

"由于这个原因,……"

(2)at all costs

"不惜任何代价"。

(3)I believe it is important to define what the flip side of not having...

"我认为去定义一下……的不利一面是很重要的"。想一想雅思题目,好多都是谈论好处与坏处的,记住这些表达,你就能"无招胜有招"!

(4)...what is required of this situation is...

"在这种情况下,需要的是……"

(5)What is important to remember is that...

"要记住的重要一点就是……"。这个句子并不难,但是好多考生在考场上却记不起来,一个名词性的句子作主语,改变自己总是用简单句的尴尬!

示范练习 21

Tourism is seen as a major industry for many countries. However, it tends to have a deleterious effect on the environment and should be strictly monitored.

To what extent do you agree or disagree with this opinion?

Tourism is vital to many world economies and depends to a certain extent on environmental protection and cultural preservation. The tourism industry like various ecological systems is complex.

In this essay I would like to explore how local communities are affected by tourism and what measures can be taken by governments and individuals to monitor and guarantee the conservation of environments of natural and historical significance.

There exist **considerable differences** between tourist and local **perceptions** of an area. Tourists are often seeing an area for the first time with a certain amount of openness and enthusiasm, whereas local residents tend to take for granted the area that they live in and often do not take the time to appreciate the unique characteristics of their hometown. This difference in perceptions suggests that local tourism officials have to be conscious of the nature of their local area. Tourism has on many occasions affected areas in the world to such an extent that local residents can no longer recognize their hometown because of overwhelming increases in population during peak seasons and large scale development in the form of hotel resorts, international chain restaurants, airports, highways and so forth.

So how can a local community pull in tourists and revenue without sacrificing its unique local flavor? First and foremost, local residents must implement **sustainable** tourism with long-term tactics for economic development and not invite the type of tourism which allows outside investors to quickly take control of an area. Sustainable tourism allows for the preservation and protection of local resources.

In reality, the more aware a community is of its unique assets, whether cultural, architectural, or natural, the more visitors it will draw.

【题目分析】

"旅游业被许多国家视为主要产业。但是这会导致严重的环境污染,应该严格禁止。从多大程度上你同意或者不同意这个看法。"首段指出这个问题复杂"complex"。2段提出全文的涵盖内容。第3段分析旅游业带来的危害。第4段提出解决方案。第5段总结。

【评分】9

【星级词汇解析】

considerable differences 巨大差异　　　　perception *n*.透彻理解

sustainable *adj*.可持续的

【万能句子解析】

(1)preservation and protection

学会这种无处不在的"万能"并列用法。

(2)In reality, the more aware a community is of its unique assets, whether cultural, architectural, or natural, the more visitors it will draw.

比较级连用！这是一个给大家示范句式多变写法的好例子。

示范练习 22

Technology is making it possible to stay at home and work.

Discuss the advantages and disadvantages of this and present your opinion on this issue.

There is a revolution going on in the developed world whereby the work-from-home dream is becoming more and more of a reality for millions of workers wishing to save time, see their families more, and achieve overall work-life equilibrium. This is made possible for many by advances in information and communications technology, namely with the advent of the Internet and mobile telecommunications such as broadband phone connections.

115

In the following paragraphs I will examine both the potential benefits and downsides of this new phenomenon which allows high-speed transmission of data from your personal computer at home to your clients and work colleagues in different locales.

It is true that computers these days have greater processing power than they did just a few years ago, but working from home is not just an issue of cost-saving. People are tired of commuting and the time spent on trains and subways is a precious commodity that could be spent more effectively on work. In many cases working from home is not actually a choice for most business executives who are accountable for business transactions around the clock.

For those people with young children, working from home has many incentives. Indeed, one could argue that a lot of **flexi-working** has **evolved** around parents' child-rearing responsibilities. However, those parents who are working from home are now experiencing new pressures in the work-from-home setting. In spite of the paybacks from less travel and more flexibility, there is a downside with increased working hours. The reality is that all home workers with children feel that balancing home and work responsibilities is easier said than done.

To make one final point, it is important when considering this **growing trend** in working from home that we do not see it as an easy option.

【题目分析】

"科技可以让人们足不出户就可以工作成为可能。请阐述其优点和缺点，并给出题,第 2 段提出文章涵盖内容。第 3 段提出分论点"working ... issue of cost-saving."第 4 段提出有小孩的人这样有好处。

应负责的	flexi-working 灵活的工作方式
evolve 发展	growing trend 增长的趋势

【万能句子解析】

(1)benefits and downsides

"好处与坏处","缺点"在英语里有许多同意表达法,这里就是一种,大家还可以用"dark side"等。"shortcoming"已经有些"落伍"了!

(2)It is true that computers these days have greater processing power than they did just a few years ago.

一个很妙的复合句!

(3)...one could argue that...

引出别人的观点的句子。

(4)To make one final point, it is important...

再熟悉一下这种承上启下引出最后一点的用法!

示范练习 23

Society is experiencing an increase in many problems such as crime and drug abuse due to urbanization.

Give some suggestions to control this trend.

Cities are growing rapidly. In a recent visit to Manchester's Urbis museum in the United Kingdom which is **devoted** to cities of the world and their development, I learned that currently almost half the world's population lives in cities and that in the next twenty to thirty years urban settings will contain up to three quarters of all humanity. However, it would seem that problems **associated with** rapid urbanization such as crime and drug abuse are growing even faster.

Notwithstanding the human **misery** that crime and **drug abuse** causes, dangerous urban areas are viewed as holding up much needed development in cities throughout the world. Investors are often unenthusiastic about **initiating** economic ventures be-

116

cause of the threat of crime and drug related violence. It goes without saying that the security of cities is vital for economic and social development, to say the least. In response to this realization <u>there is a growing trend</u> in urban planning in some countries which is taking aim at **wide-scale** problems like crime and **narcotics abuse.**

Urban design professionals are now being consulted to identify areas of urban planning which will endorse security. **<u>Recreational</u> programs** for residents living in crime-ridden areas, and advice on housing management and sanitation are some of the solutions being proposed by city planners for those citizens wanting to live in safer communities. Urban developers are also looking to remodel downtrodden public spaces which are havens for criminal activity by making them more beautiful and by inspiring a sense of pride in local inhabitants.

As far as I can see, planners and developers who consult residents **systematically** about changes in store for the development of problematic urban areas have a far greater chance at success. By keeping those residents informed, who will benefit directly from plans for urban restructuring to reduce crime, will instill a sense of responsibility which is often absent in urban communities.

【题目分析】

"城市化带来越来越多诸如犯罪和吸毒之类的问题。请给出控制这个趋势的方法。"这是一个与一般题目不同的 topic,要求考生给出解决办法。看一下雅思考官是如何处理的。首段引出主题。第 2 段提出城市潜在的问题。第 3 段提出解决方法 "urban design …"。第 4 段总结。

【评分】9

【星级词汇解析】

devote vt. 投入于	be associated with 和……相关
notwithstanding prep. 尽管	misery n. 苦楚
drug abuse 吸毒	initiate v. 开始
narcotics abuse 吸毒(此毒与 drug 稍微不同,实际上是做了个同义转换)	
recreational adj. 娱乐的	systematically adv. 系统地

【万能句子解析】

There is a growing trend...

"……有增长的势头"

示范练习 24

With the development of modern science and technology, some aspects of traditional culture are being lost, and some people now believe that traditional cultures will eventually be replaced by modern science and technology such as computers and the Internet.

What is your opinion on this matter?

Digital information technologies are **symbolic** of the **dominant** global culture that is currently taking our world by storm. Due to developments in modern science and technology, traditional ways of earning a living, learning something new and even that of existing are rapidly transforming. This transformation in the way we communicate and live is as significant as the invention of writing which **altered** the course of **ancient** cultures before us.

Nevertheless, up-to-the-minute technologies have the capacity to preserve many aspects of traditional culture. Indeed, if we are to employ information and communications technologies effectively, traditional values and **ethics** can help us make decisions for the proper use of these new technologies. In this essay I will explore how the negative impact of the Internet on traditional cultures and values can be **lessened** through awareness-raising exchanges and education.

In most parts of the world government authorities reacted to the introduction of the World Wide Web by prohibiting unlimited access to all Internet sites. They argued that some content found on the Internet would **jeopardize** traditional cultural and religious values. In the last few years, however, although this issue is still hotly debated among the powers that be, we are now seeing bans lifted on Internet access in all corners of the world.

The Internet is changing traditional cultures by offering users new means for voicing their opinions about everything, including politics, religion, and love. For example, in the United Arab Emirates where the two sexes are firmly **segregated**, the Internet is enabling men and women to communicate in new ways that were not permissible before. Additionally, as a communications medium the Internet is allowing traditional values to be heard alongside more unconventional values as users face up to different ideas and hear other people's opinions.

The networking and awareness-raising potential offered by computers and the Internet about different cultures and values is unlimited. Now that we have people from more traditional cultures communicating online it is almost assured that their values and beliefs will be more readily heard and respected by the **all-encompassing** global Internet community.

【题目分析】

"随着现代科技的发展,传统文化的某些方面必然会失去。有人认为传统文化最终将被电脑等现代科技代替。你的观点是什么?"首段提出科技确实在改变一些东西,第 2 段马上提出但是科技也能保留传统文化的许多方面。第 3 段举例说科技(网络)会有负面的东西而且仍有该被禁止的地方。第 4 段再次指出因特网实际上促进传统文化的传播。第 5 段总结。

【评分】9

119

【星级词汇解析】

symbolic *adj*. 象征的, 符号的   dominant *adj*. 占优势的, 支配的

alter *v*. 改变   ancient *adj*. 远古的, 旧的

ethics *n*. 道德规范   lessen *v*. 减少, 减轻

jeopardize *v*. 危害   segregate *v*. 隔离

all-encompassing *adj*. 包罗万象的

【万能句子解析】

(1) **transforming** 与 **This transformation** 同义转换,万能妙用!

(2) In most parts of the world government authorities...

"in most parts of the world"这种用法很常见。

(3) They argued that...

引出某部分人的观点。

(4) In the last few years, however...

实现巧妙承接的好句子。

(5) ...in all corners of the world.

大家往往愿意用"世界每一个地方/角落",但表达却常犯错,现在该记住了!

示范练习 25

Some sporting events such as the World Cup may help reduce tension and bias between different countries and promote peace in the world.

To what extent do you agree or disagree with this opinion?

Recently the media announced FIFA's (Federation of International Football Association) decision to hold the 2010 World Cup Games in South Africa which will be a first for the continent of Africa. This is the world's most **prestigious** football tournament and it means all the world's attention will be turned on South Africa for a month of international sporting glory.

The previous World Cup Games were jointly held in Korea and Japan which was also a first for Asia. In this essay, I will look at how relations between the two Koreas, Japan and the US were improved because of the 2002 World Cup and how this has a direct effect on promoting world peace.

First of all, I would like to mention that FIFA's decision has not gone without criticism in South Africa; as rising unemployment and wide-scale poverty are still among the most urgent problems facing South Africa. This is the downside of the World Cup as it is an extremely expensive tournament to host. Nonetheless, it will be a time for South Africans to celebrate 10 years of democracy and the end of **apartheid** which has already lessened tension and bias toward South Africa from the outside world.

The effect the World Cup had on diplomatic relations between Japan and South Korea cannot be underestimated. Likewise, small steps were made in the direction of resuming long-**suspended** talks between Tokyo and Pyongyang and this greatly pleased the US and the United Nations. Although longer-ranging effects remain to be seen, the 2002 World Cup made advances in world peace and North Korea took great pride in South Korea's achievement in the quarter finals.

The way has been opened for South Africa to follow suit in 2010. Already, South Korea and Japan can look back with **approval** on the first World Cup ever hosted in Asia as one of the most **exhilarating** and spirited in modern history, with no incidents of terrorism or **hooliganism**.

【题目分析】

"一些体育赛事,如世界杯,可以减少国家间的紧张和偏见,让世界更和平。从多大程度上你同意或者不同意这种观点。"首段引入主题。第2段用一个例子说明确实如此。第3段让步,提出体育赛事并不是没有遭到批评。第4段正面论述好处。第5段总结,展望。

【评分】9

120

【星级词汇解析】

prestigious *adj.* 享有声望的，声望很高的	apartheid *n.* （南非)种族隔离
suspended *adj.* 暂停的	approval *n.* 赞成
exhilarating *adj.* 令人喜欢的	hooliganism *n.* 流氓行为

示范练习 26

Some people think that if one wants to succeed in life, then one must have a formal university education.

To what extent do you agree or disagree with this opinion?

The ancient Chinese **sage**, **Confucius**, is renowned for his **adages** and he had many things to say about living and learning. The following quotation from Confucius may shed light on this essay question: "Study without thinking and you are blind; think without studying and you are in danger."

Most people would agree that everyone receives a general education through the experiences that life offers them. Some of us—the more **privileged**—engage in formal schooling which is one of the many ways of gaining an education. In its ideal form, formal education imparts knowledge and contextual understanding of the world we live in. Through courses of study we can **be exposed to** ideas that we may not have **come across** ourselves; for more often than not, the culture of learning has been created by individuals and cultures that have preceeded us or by those who are situated far from our present location.

In this increasingly global world, standards are being set for education whereby those who hold university degrees often receive greater privileges in life in terms of the status they are given, the work they can perform and the money they can earn. In no other time in history have we witnessed such a drive toward higher learning by countries the world over to achieve economies of knowledge.

This emphasis on formal schooling also serves as a great frustration for some students enrolled in higher education, as the courses of study they are on do not always arouse their true passions and curiosity for learning. The quandary of how to best educate students has always rested on the matter of giving students the freedom to discover knowledge for themselves versus the controlled transmission of knowledge received on taught courses.

121

In order to truly succeed in life, formal education is important for getting ahead but so is your ability to be able to share what you know with others who can benefit from your lived and learned experience.

【题目分析】

"有人认为如果想要成功,必须接受正规的大学教育。从多大程度上你同意或者不同意这种观点。"首段末句用名言引入主题:受教育也要动脑,否则也不行! 第 2 段提出学校教育确实有用,第 3 段进一步论证这一点。第 4 段指出没有动脑思考的过程,教育也会有折扣的。第 5 段总结。

【评分】9

【星级词汇解析】

sage *adj*. 贤明的 *n*. 贤人 　　　　Confucius *n*. 孔子

adage *n*. 格言,谚语 　　　　　　　privilege *n*. 特权

be exposed to 接触到 　　　　　　come across 遇到

【万能句子解析】

(1) In this increasingly global world, standards...

这是一个泛泛到几乎任何文章都可以借用的句子了。

(2) In no other time in history have we witnessed such a drive toward...

这里 drive 是名词用法,意思是"强劲的趋势",作者很喜欢这个句子,"历史没有任何时候像现在这样,有……趋势/潮流!"莫等闲,白了少年头,空悲切! 顺历史而动吧,同学们!

(3) This emphasis on formal schooling also serves as...

把 formal schooling 一改,马上就"万能"!

(4) passions and curiosity

"热情与好奇"。

emphasB

emphasB on

示范练习 27

Some people think that developed countries should fund international aid to poor countries to help developing countries improve domestic health, education and trade.

To what extent do you agree or disagree with this opinion?

First of all, to discuss this statement effectively, it might be helpful to determine exactly what development means. In its most general sense, development means change and most people would agree on this point. However, when it comes to discussing development in more precise terms, things become more difficult.

To take an obvious example: a country whose gross national product (GNP) is rising in the area of trade exports may not be developing in terms of health and education. The rise in GNP may only be a reflection of the greater than before production and sale of a naturally occurring resource such as crude oil or other raw materials.

In particular, what I would like to point out is that the term, economic development, is all too often used interchangeably with development, yet it only implies the transformation of a country's economy. True development, on the other hand, denotes the course of economic and social transformation within a country. This is what developed countries have over developing countries in terms of improved standards in humanwelfare; higher levels of education, superior health care, a longer life expectancy, and an increase in domestic food consumption. This in turn begs the question of what role foreign aid should play in promoting economic advancement and improved standards in human welfare among developing countries.

Personally, I fully sanction the continued supply of international funding from developed nations to developing countries as there have been numerous accounts where this aid has achieved real results. To give an example, South Korea, a country which I have spent a lot of time in over the last decade, and Taiwan were both aid recipients once upon a time; now they are aid donors. In stark contrast, other countries, despite significant inflows of international funding, have not thrived and have instead fallen prey to severe poverty, civil strife, and complete political pandemonium.

Therefore, success of foreign aid often lies with the current political climate and the policies of the recipient as well as the aid policies of the donor.

【题目分析】

"有人认为发达国家应该资助贫穷国家,以便帮助发展中国家来发展健康、教育、和贸易事业等。从多大程度上你同意或者不同意这种观点。"首段提出就字面而言,很难界定发达的标准。第2段进一步说明这一点。第3、4段给出作者观点,同意富国资助穷国。最后总结。

【评分】9

【万能句子解析】

(1)...most people would agree on this point.

"大部分人都认为",引出观点的常用句式。

(2)...when it comes to discussing...

123

"当谈到……时"

(3)In particular, what I would like to point out is that…

陈述自己观点的万能句式！

(4)Personally, I fully sanction. . *sanction*

sanction 表示"同意"，绝对比 agree 拿分，有分量的词汇！

(5)In stark contrast. . .

"鲜明对照"，表示比较的时候万能使用！

示范练习 28

Should developing countries only concentrate on improving industrial skills and modern technology or should they promote education first?

Present your opinion.

When we look at education in many developing parts of the world we can **discern** that it is at a difficult crossroads. This is especially true in the least developed countries. There exists a **two-pronged** pressure on the education sector to meet economies' growing demands for highly skilled and trained workers, along with the need to continue the **expansion** of knowledge.

More often than not, a litany of problems faces educational institutions in the developing world including inadequate budgeting from governments, **spiraling** resource costs, rapidly increasing student numbers, and large illiterate populations. Due to the scale of these problems, many governments are trying to **weigh up** the apparent advantages and disadvantages of improving literacy rates against the need to increase industrial productivity.

Access to the latest technologies is usually what divides developed nations from their developing sister nations. Interestingly, while the burden of **mounting** public spending on education is a fact of life in many developing countries; on-line distance education is becoming an important way to address many of the concerns confronting the majority of mankind. New Information and communications technologies (ICT) are creating **remarkable** shifts in societies all over the world. Ironically, it will be through increased computer literacy which in turn aids linguistic literacy that the developing world will see its largest returns in education and industry.

In many respects, if developing countries were to promote education first, then several of the objectives of computer-based distance education could be realized. Online education would help widen overall access to education, raise the value of education through training and by making resources available, and bring about new methods and approaches for teaching and learning. Through this new and improved computerized route in education at a fraction of the cost of traditional education, developing countries will be able to achieve and sustain considerable gains in their overall welfare.

【题目分析】

"发展中国家应该只注重提高工业技能和现代科技,还是应该首先倡导教育。给出你的观点。"首段引入主题,没陈述观点。第2段论述教育面临的问题。第3段指出科技使发达和发展中国家有差距。第4段提出解决办法,即作者观点。

【评分】9

【星级词汇解析】

discern v. 辨别   two-pronged adj. 分两端的

expansion n. 扩充   spiraling adj. 螺旋形的

weigh up 重要性(等)······超过   mounting adj. 越来越多的

【万能句子解析】

(1)More often than not, a litany of problems faces...

"经常会出现的一种现象······",引述一种事物时候的万能句子!

(2)In many respects, if developing countries were to promote education...

"在许多方面,······"

示范练习 29

Does modern technology make life more convenient, or was life better when technology was simpler?

What is your opinion?

It is difficult to think how we managed our lives before the **widespread** use of everyday technologies such as the Internet and mobile phones which we now take for granted. Despite this, how often do we stop to question ourselves, before going online to check our email accounts, whether modern technology has really made our lives more convenient? Some people may actually answer to the contrary, that modern technology has made their lives more complicated and even more difficult.

The obvious advantages of modern-day technologies are many. For example, if I do not want to go home and wash my **laundry** and wait for the weather to clear so I can hang it outside to dry, I simply invest in a machine that can both wash and dry my clothes. In addition, I would feel safer in the knowledge that because my clothes are not hanging up outside the possibility of them being stolen is greatly reduced.

Inventors throughout the ages have thought of practically every device imaginable to assist humans in conducting their everyday affairs, from baby strollers to life-support machines. In fact, we are inundated with technological contraptions in this modern world and there is no sign of a reversal in this trend occurring.

Imagine for a moment, if there were no televisions or computers. How would you know who had won the latest soccer match? Or what was going on in the news? What would the weather be like tomorrow? The problem with modern technology is not the unlimited choices in **gadgetry** now made available to us; but instead, it is our increasing inability to tune out from an overload in information and our growing reliance on machines that perform mindless tasks which we could simply do for ourselves.

The use of modern technology does **inspire** inventors, designers and engineers to **speculate on** what technology will be like in the future and how it could further mankind's survival and development. However, before we turn around and say technology is the best thing that ever happened to us, it is vital that we remember who is in control of technology in order for it not to take over our lives completely.

【题目分析】

"现代科技真的使生活更方便了吗? 还是说在过去技术比较简单的时候生活更好一些呢? 你怎么看?"首段分析两方面,提出不同人的观点。第 2 段分析好处,第 3、4 段进一步阐述好处。最后总结,并圆滑地在最后做了个小让步,使文章无懈可击!

【评分】9

【星级词汇解析】

    widespread *adj*. 普遍的

    laundry *n*. 洗衣店(曾想过把这样的词汇用在写作里吗? 如果你的回答是 No, 那从现在开始行动!)

    gadgetry *n*. 小配件,小玩意

    speculate *vi*. 推测,思索

    inspire *vt*. 鼓舞

【万能句子解析】

    (1)Some people may actually answer to the contrary...

陈述出另外一派人的观点的万能用法。

(2)The obvious advantages of modern-day technologies are many.

"明显的优点……"

(3)How would you know who had won the latest soccer match? Or what was going on in the news? What would the weather be like tomorrow?

这3个排山倒海的句子,大家一定要记住,并用在你的文章里!

(4)growing reliance on

"越来越多的依赖于……"

(5)...inventors, designers and engineers to speculate on...

speculate 表示"考虑"的意思。

示范练习 30 Report

Fresh drinking water is becoming a scarce and all too expensive commodity in many parts of the world.

Discuss the causes and give suggestions for how to ensure adequate water supply for the world's inhabitants.

The words of Samuel Taylor Coleridge are revealing when we ponder the issue of water scarcity: "Water, water everywhere", as the Ancient Mariner said, "Nor any drop to drink".

It would seem that one of the biggest threats to supplies of fresh drinking water is that, at least in the rich West, it is largely taken for granted. In any case, it is the most frequently-occurring substance with most of the earth's surface being covered in H_2O.

Our toughest challenge of the 21st century may not be **pandemic diseases** such as AIDS or the threat of nuclear war, but may in fact turn out to be a lack of fresh water. If we are not careful, the possibility of water wars in the future may outstrip our reasons for warring on nations who control other naturally occurring resources such as oil.

At present many people lack access to clean water and even more people lack access to proper **sanitation**; nearly all of them reside in developing countries. A continuation in population growth, environmental pollution and climatic changes are all likely to contribute to a **devastating** decline in water supply in the coming years. Similarly, with rapid urbanization occurring all over, the possibility for concentrated waste matter to reach unmanageable proportions is also highly likely in many regions.

Unless we take **affirmative** action to properly conserve and manage the world's fresh water supplies, the effects of water scarcity will undoubtedly affect human health and the chances for survival for all of the earth's inhabitants. Water-related diseases caused by **ingesting contaminated water** and vector-borne diseases, such as malaria, are spread by insects that use water to breed. Raising much needed awareness about the importance of fresh water supplies and what we can do to further conserve this precious resource will become a top priority to everyone if we wish to survive.

【题目分析】

"在世界范围内,饮用水正在变成一种稀缺而又昂贵的商品。讨论造成这些的原因,并提出建议,如何确保世界居民的水供应。"前两段引入主题。第3段提出面临的问题。第4段进一步分析这个问题。第5段提出解决建议。行文结构非常清晰。

【评分】 9

【星级词汇解析】

pandemic disease 流行性疾病   sanitation *n*. 卫生,卫生设施

devastating *adj*. 破坏性的, 全然的   affirmative *adj*. 肯定的

ingesting contaminated water 饮用受污染的水

【万能句子解析】

(1)It would seem that...

"似乎……"。

(2)Our toughest challenge of the 21st century may not be...

这是个每一篇文章开始都可以使用的万能句子!

必考雅思写作真题分析及未来考试题目预测

We are here to add what we can to life, not to get what we can from it.

我们要尽可能为生活增加一些东西,而不是从中索取什么。

——*William Osler* 奥斯勒

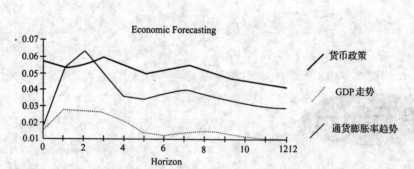

There are two groups of people you are likely to hear each night making predictions on the evening news: Meteorologists who forecast the atmospheric weather, telling us if we should expect rain, sunshine or snow and Economists who, on the other hand, predict the financial "weather", forecasting whether we should expect a recession, inflation or unemployment in the upcoming weeks and months.

—*Virginia Department of Education*

确实,世界上有两类人最喜欢预测:一类是气象学家,而另一类则是经济学家。2003 年,诺贝尔经济学奖得主罗伯特·恩格尔(Robert F. Engle)和克莱夫·格兰杰(Clive WJ Granger)的贡献就是对金融、股票市场的发展情况作出的预测(forecasting),从这一世界顶级经济学大奖给予的肯定我们就可以看出,预测在现实生活中用途也颇为广泛。笔者虽然在经济学这个博大精深的学科中学习实践了几年,虽然绝不能以经济学家自居,但是多年在英国教授雅思课程和与雅思考官共事的经验,却可以有把握地对雅思作文题目的出题趋势和题目内容有一个到位的预测。

这一部分给出 10 篇未来大家在现场会遇到(完全类似)的真题文章,所有文章题目都是笔者根据出题规律精挑细选并加工出来的。而给出的范文更是凝聚了笔者长时间的心血,希望大家有所收获,能真正突破雅思作文议论文写作关。

为了方便大家更快更好地把握要点,我们在范文之前对题目进行了分析,这样可以方便大家更快地在脑海里形成一个对题目大概内容的印象(a general picture)。然后再查看万能范文部分,进行写作模仿。大家可以花一定的时间把提供的主题内容稍做修改,加以牢记,在考试中必定屡试不爽。

为了提高效率,下文先给大家列出了精选文章的目录,我们略去大家已经很熟悉的常规要求内容(You should write at least 250 words. Use your own knowledge and experience and support your arguments with examples and relevant evidence.)以节省篇幅,但给出字数供大家参考。大家可以根据需要有选择地进行阅读。正如大家备考雅思一样,一切都要提高效率,快速高效地学好雅思写作!

提醒:下列题目都是最近、最新历次国内外雅思考试考过的,也是于雅思题库中取题并会出现在未来考试中的题目,这里给的范文大家可以结合第四部分的范文融汇成"自己的"文章,这样就可以在考场上游刃有余,以不变应万变,40分钟完成一篇文章,对大家来说就是小菜一碟儿(a piece of cake)!

真题题目预测万能范文 10 篇

示范练习 1

Nowadays there are many doctors specializing in profitable activities such as plastic surgery and private health care for privileged patients. Should doctors, however, be concentrating more on the general public's health, regardless of how rich patients may be?

Respond with your own opinion.

【题目分析】

"时下许多医生从事于一些很赚钱的活动,比如整形手术或者是为一些有特权的人做私人医生。但是医生是不是应该更多地关注普通大众的身体健康,而不论病人有多富有呢? 请谈谈你的观点。"

In most societies doctors are treated with a great deal of respect and there is a vast amount of evidence to support why this is so. First of all, they have dedicated themselves to the medical profession through extended periods of highly rigorous and taxing training. Secondly, the hours they put in at hospitals and clinics are often grueling, and thirdly, the responsibility they have in caring for patients with a multiplicity of health complaints is immerse.

In many cases doctors are miracle workers in the way that they manage to save lives; although in most cases, I would say that doctors are overworked and that their health may be suffering due to high levels of job-related stress. In my response to the above statement, I would like to emphasize that in the majority of situations doctors around the world are doing their best to serve the general public with the resources made available to them.

Nevertheless, in the past decade we have observed a significant surge in the cosmetic surgery industry, especially in developed countries where it is mostly performed on women. This sudden growth in the popularity of plastic surgery has not occurred without criticism, however. Due to the amount of money to be made in cosmetic surgery some doctors are attempting to make a financial killing out of the situation by focusing their energies on this one area alone. As a result, concerns have been raised about the medical background of some doctors, limited regulations and the likelihood of dangerous procedures, along with overkill in money-making promotions. To a larger extent, with this rising trend in catering for the rich, there has been public criticism of the entire medical establishment.

It goes without saying, however, that doctors like most professionals are more liable to improve patient care when they are encouraged with incentives such as public acknowledgment, improved working conditions and access to proper clinical information systems. Provided these requirements are in place, patients would be more likely to receive the attention, trust and personal care that they seek in a medical practitioner.

My final point, therefore, rests with government spending in the area of public health in providing people with the medical services they require while taking care of the professional needs of doctors.

示范练习 2

With the development of market economies advertising has become a dominant

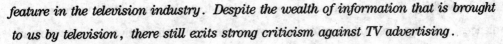
feature in the television industry. Despite the wealth of information that is brought to us by television, there still exits strong criticism against TV advertising.

What is your opinion?

【题目分析】

"随着市场经济的发展,广告已经成为电视行业的主要特点。尽管电视为我们提供了许多信息,但是对电视广告仍存在强烈的批评。你的观点是什么?"

For the past several decades, advertising on TV has been at the center of heated debate from both within and outside the entertainment and advertising sectors. In no other time in history have we seen a form of entertainment that is so widely accessible to the masses. Oftentimes, television is the only type of entertainment that underprivileged families can afford and it is not unusual to find TV in some of the world's remotest areas. Notably, children make up a major part of any television audience, a fact that TV advertisers are well aware of. In this essay, I will investigate some of the adverse effects television advertising has on viewers within market economies around the globe. Television has its benefits of which we are all conscious, and no one could deny that it is an educative tool for audiences, especially young viewers. However, television is also a form of communications mass media and is often employed as a manipulative tool by many advertisers working in industry.

In fact, TV advertisers are well aware that children are captive audiences who are vulnerable to the hard sell, the flashy images, and the recurring images that implant messages into their receptive minds. Research has shown that there is a direct association between television commercials for junk foods, snacks and candies and mounting levels of obesity among children.

Excessive consumption is the hard and fast result of television advertising in market economies all over the world. Researchers are also concerned that TV advertising places excessive pressure on men and women to center undue attention on their appearance. An overemphasis on the importance of physical attractiveness in an attempt to sell products at all costs is another feature of advertising on TV. Many men and women now fear being unattractive or old because of the information relayed to them through television advertising.

133

In addition to the points raised above, television advertising is intrusive into audiences, viewing time. How often have you found yourself captivated by a program on TV to be interrupted by a bombardment of unwanted commercials? Governments should therefore ensure that the amount of television advertising time is kept to a minimum, as it is more often than not an unwanted nuisance factor in our modern market-driven lives. In their hearts, I believe people just want to be able to relax in front of a television.

示范练习3

Nowadays we are seeing more and more exhibitions and sculptures appearing in public places. It is wrong that governments are funding artist projects when there are more important things we could be doing with tax payers' money.

To what extent do you agree or disagree with this opinion?

【题目分析】

"当今时代,我们在公共场所看到越来越多的展览和雕塑。当纳税人缴纳的税金还有更重要的用途的时候,政府却用来资助艺术项目! 从多大程度上你同意或者是不同意这个观点?"

Some people question whether arts projects should be publicly funded by any means, refuting that governments should not be collecting tax-payers' money to support exhibitions and public sculptures that many people do not visit or appreciate. Instead, they believe that the arts ought to be patronized by devoted fans, as sporting events are, or by way of confidential philanthropy.

Even so, in some regions of the world vast amounts of arts funding is being disbursed by local governing bodies, indicating that there is support for the arts. We need to question why this is so, and of what benefit communities see artist projects being. By way of forming my own opinion to the assigned statement, I will discuss the many virtues of artist projects for the continuation and development of unique world cultures.

It can be argued that the arts significantly affect societies on several specific and important levels. First and foremost, art can create a sense of social cohesion as people identify with the work of local artists, past and present. Art also serves to educate and preserve local traditions, and can even spur on economic development by way of promoting the tourism industry. Most sight-seeing in the world is based around art objects and art performances as art is central to culture.

In addition, reports have shown that children who participate in the arts often perform better in their main school subjects. For example, children who are exposed to music from a very young age often do better in mathematics. Finally, it is important to remember that skills fostered through creativity are valued highly in places of work.

As I mentioned earlier, the arts can create a vibrant sector within local and national economies. Arts and culture are closely intertwined with industry within most market economies around the world. The mass-production of tourist souvenirs, jewelry, clothing, and furniture are but a few examples of how art has created a boon in industry. Thus, for many, art has value not only for art's sake but for the state of their economy as well.

135

示范练习 4

Students who go directly from school to university benefit less from, and contribute less to their courses than those who take a job or travel in order to get more experience in the "real world" before starting higher education.

To what extent do you agree or disagree with this statement?

【题目分析】

"那些从中学一毕业就升入大学的学生,他们从大学课程里的受益和对学科的贡献都没有那些在上大学之前为了从"现实世界"获得更多经验而去工作和旅游的人多。你从多大程度上同意或者是不同意这种说法?"

Taking a gap year between finishing high school and entering tertiary education is widely recognized as beneficial, and the variety of things one can do overwhelms some young people. Nevertheless, I am thoroughly in support of the above statement and will endeavor to exemplify my opinion on this matter throughout the following discussion.

Increasingly, gap years are being utilized to earn qualifications in activities that the younger generation might otherwise have no time for. Instructor courses in skiing and scuba diving, for example, are a great way to enjoy a popular pastime and still come out with an actual qualification. Likewise, arts and language courses are less physical alternatives, but they offer invaluable inroads into intercultural communications and increased understanding of international relations.

With the job market becoming increasingly more competitive, there are many career-minded young people who are looking for ways to make their year out count by gaining "real world" experience. Indeed, there has been rapid growth within the area of gap year internships and this is positively encouraged by universities, and employers who are looking for someone who has picked up some worthwhile experience while away from home.

I think that people's understanding of gap years has changed dramatically in the last few years as being something more structured as opposed to just taking an extended vacation. The structured gap year activities that are most commonly selected by youths can be broken down into the following three main areas: development work usually in Third World regions; language learning courses or getting qualified in a skill that can later be taught, for instance sky diving; and last but not the least, volunteer work, both at home and abroad.

The important thing to remember here is that when students decide to take a year out that this decision does not equate to taking a year off. Yes, gap years should be enjoyable but they should also include goals that will later contribute to future university courses and careers.

示范练习 5

Modern technology has had a great influence on people's entertainment choices, making them less creative.

Do you agree or disagree with this opinion?

【题目分析】

"现代科技对人们的娱乐有巨大的影响,使得人们缺乏创造性。你是否同意这种观点?"

There exist many different types of entertainment technologies which cause us to behave in a variety of ways. Television, for example, only requires passive viewing and listening and can be looked upon as a form of entertainment which dulls the mind. The Internet, on the other hand, requires users to be interactive through the employment of, for example, different motoring skills i.e. clicking, selecting text etc., to more challenging tasks such as searching, emailing, chatting, and the up-loading/downloading of software. A lot of people are still choosing television as their preferred entertainment for relaxing after a hard day's work, but even more people are getting excited about the on-line world as they discover what it can do for them.

The irony of this essay question is that without creativity we would not have the modern technology that we use today. We would not have television or the Internet. Similarly, we would not have MP3 players or DVDs. Every invention known to mankind has always resulted from creative thinking. Arguably, creativity is our most important asset; and information is an inestimable tool. With no electronic databases, PCs, and other supportive networking technology, we would be hard pressed to orga-nize all of our information efficiently and effectively.

However, if we examine the example of the Internet closer, we can also discern that the quantity of information on-line is escalating at a staggering rate. This means that it is difficult for individuals to remain up-to-date in their chosen fields. Due to this increasing pressure in the working world, it is therefore necessary for people to band together, to work collaboratively, and to think creatively and imaginatively to thrive and even to survive.

In conclusion, I would like to add that the days of choosing modern technology purely for entertainment purposes are diminishing. It is no longer enough to merely own modern gadgetry. Instead, you must be able to show that you can manipulate technology creatively to suit your every purpose.

137

The primary use for creative technologies is problem solving, and this requires users to adopt both divergent and convergent thinking processes. On the one hand, creativity generates a vast potential of new possibilities, whereas on the other hand, creativity begins by taking many new ideas and drawing them together to form a single objective. Who knows what entertainment possibilities are in store for us just around the corner? Try to imagine!

示范练习 6

138

Some people say that older people should live with their adult children, while others think that they should live in homes specially built for old people.

Which do you think is better practice?

【题目分析】

"有人认为老人应该住在年长的孩子那里,也有人觉得老人应该住在专门为老人建的公寓里。你认为哪种方式更合理?"

These days, it is difficult to say whether the practice of living alone or with one's adult children is more amicable for the elderly. This would depend entirely on the relationship between members within a particular family to determine which option is more suitable. However, I can say that the traditional practice of the extended family where elderly people enjoy love and respect from their family members in addition to food, clothing and shelter appears to be diminishing to a great extent.

In this essay, I will examine some of the reasons for this change in the following discussion. In recent times, several factors have created a great impact on family structuring; the replacement of extended families with nuclear families, choosing to have fewer children due to rising population and economic pressures, an increase in the number of women who go out to work, and the migration of younger family members to cities to find better paying jobs. For those senior citizens caught up in these changing times, expectations that they may have had for their twilight years are now shifting.

Family solidarity is valued by most people in every society, therefore it is natural that caring responsibilities between generations should be brought forward for consideration. In our increasingly urbanized world, the occurrence of old people's homes and silver towns is becoming more commonplace.

Living independently from one's adult children and one's extended family often requires a lot more autonomy and decision-making in later life. Many grey-haired individuals possess their full mental and physical faculties until they are very old and are quite capable of looking after themselves. Others, however, are not so fortunate and are therefore more dependent on family members and professional care-givers.

What remains true, for elderly people living alone or with their families, is that people's attitudes toward senior citizens have to change in order to promote active citizenship for elderly people. Even in our modern industrialized societies we have to make older people feel valued so they are not looked upon as a liability by their families or their communities.

139

示范练习 7

Some people say that sports should not be encouraged in schools because they cause competition rather than cooperation among students.

To what extent do you agree or disagree with this opinion?

【题目分析】

"有人认为学校里不应该鼓励体育运动,因为体育运动造成学生间的竞争,而不是合作。从多大程度上你同意或者不同意这种观点?"

As a direct response to this question, I would like to suggest that an element of healthy competition between students is constructive in most cases. However, having the opportunity to participate in a sporting event is more important than winning for a variety of reasons which I will present in this discussion. Competitive sports, as we all know, promote good sportsmanship in their ideal form. It follows, therefore, that school-aged children have a far greater chance of developing social competencies if they have been schooled from an early age in how to be a "good sport".

Countless hours of play and sporting competition between students helps to develop an array of skills. They range from the obvious physical competencies, i. e. how to throw a ball, how to hit, and how to catch, all the way to appreciating the associated benefits of fairness, inclusiveness, cooperation, respect for others in spite of their sporting ability, and the importance of having fun.

Apart from developing greater diplomacy between students, competitive sports also help young people to create a positive self-image and to take a keen interest in their health and fitness. This is extremely valuable in our consumer-centered lives where obesity among children is continually on the increase.

Another valuable point to consider is that competitive sporting events always have a winning and losing side, so learning to deal with both success and disappointment is vital. When the pressure is on, the outcome of a sports game could go either way so it is important for students to control their emotions when frustrating situations arise. Furthermore, when poor sportsmanship is displayed, students should be reminded that there will be consequences for such behavior.

At the end of a pressured and highly competitive sporting event if both sides can shake hands with their opponents in a civilized manner then we can say that a great deal has been achieved.

示范练习 8

Since World War II there has been an increase in cooperation between many Eastern and Western countries. This has led to a desire amongst students to undertake study in foreign countries. Some people believe that this will bring advantages to students while others propose that this will cause some problems.

What do you think about this issue?

【题目分析】

"二战之后,东西方国家间的合作增多了。这也刺激了学生出国留学。有人认为这能给学生带来好处,也有人反对这种观点。你怎么看待出国留学的?"

An abundance of benefits from studying abroad have been commended by many an international student. The attractions include:practical life skills and the development of self-reliance, the chance to learn about another culture, the advancement of foreign language acquisition, work experience abroad, commencement or fulfillment of course work, exposure to new academic pursuits and developing perspectives on one's educational background, along with opportunities to make new friends and to see new places.

Access to the world is the study abroad initiative of many students today and of many higher learning institutions around the world. However, I think this is quite a recent trend in education exchanges between the East and the West.

As an English language teacher working primarily in North East Asia and in the United Kingdom, I have noticed a dramatic increase in the number of Asian students studying in Western countries over the last five years. Prior to that time, most foreign students studying in Britain, for example, were from EU countries or other English speaking regions of the world. Nowadays, we are witnessing something quite spectacular, in terms of the number of Asian students studying in countries where English is the first language, namely Britain, Canada and the United States, Australia and New Zealand. Predominantly, these students are coming from China and India, two of the world's most up and coming economies.

It is also predicted that there will be more overseas postgraduate rather than undergraduate students studying in English speaking countries as many international applicants already have a first degree from their own country. This is highly profitable for those countries giving student visas to international students. Whether this will be beneficial for those students coming from abroad and the development of their homelands is yet to be seen. Nevertheless, the spirit of determination and optimism I have observed in my Chinese students here in the UK is unbeatable.

Change is inevitable it would seem. All too frequently I have heard the aspirations of many of my overseas students for the positive contributions they would like to make in their home countries after the completion of their studies abroad.

示范练习 9

In certain countries children are not allowed to leave school until they reach a certain age, for example, in some countries it is 15 years. Write an essay expressing your point of view on the following topic: Should there be a minimum school leaving age, or should students and their parents be free to decide when they leave school?

【题目分析】

"在某些国家,小孩子只有到了一定的年龄才可以离开学校。那么是不是应该设定一个离开学校的最低年龄,还是说这个问题应该留给学生和家长们自主决定?请陈述一下你的看法和观点。"

One feature of improved education systems around the world has been an increase in the period of compulsory schooling for students. In many developed countries students are now required to stay at school until they are 15 years of age. There are quite plausible reasons for opposing this policy.

First of all, low income families, for example, may not be able to afford to keep their children at school and may resent governments, imposing this decision on them. In many developing countries, children can bring in much needed income, either by working in family agricultural activities, or else through paid employment. Compulsory schooling might also be opposed on educational grounds. Recent studies have shown that compulsory schooling can be psychologically damaging for students who are not motivated to learn. They may be more ready to learn later on as adults when their motivation is stronger.

But there are also strong reasons why students should be obliged to remain at school until a certain age. First, at a young age students are unlikely to be sufficiently mature to make sensible decisions about their lives. We should not allow students to make decisions they may later regret. A second reason is that in today's society, where increasingly high levels of skills and knowledge are required of the work force, early school leavers will find it very difficult to obtain employment.

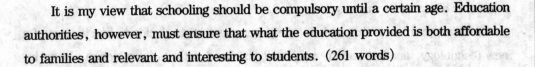

It is my view that schooling should be compulsory until a certain age. Education authorities, however, must ensure that what the education provided is both affordable to families and relevant and interesting to students. (261 words)

示范练习 10

Technology can bring many benefits, but it can also cause social and environmental problems. In relation to new technology, the primary duty of governments should be to focus on potential problems, rather than benefits.

Please discuss the issues raised here and offer your opinion.

【题目分析】

"科技能带来许多好处,但同时也会造成社会和环境问题。就新技术来讲,政府应该主要盯住潜在的问题,而不是带来的益处。请谈谈你的观点。"(这个题目和第 1 题极其相似。)

It is true that new technologies can create serious social and environmental problems. The question is whether governments should focus on these problems when they are formulating policies related to new technology.

Some people would argue that governments have an important watchdog role to play and that they should attempt to establish whether a proposed technology is likely to have any harmful effects. This is seen as an aspect of government looking after public interests and showing concern for the welfare of its citizens. These are the same people who have invested the government with the power to veto the introduction of certain technologies.

The problem with this approach, however, is that it is very difficult to know in advance what the full effects of any new technology will be. The history of science and technology has many fascinating examples of unexpected developments. Sometimes a technological advance in one area can lead to a surprising breakthrough in another, seemingly unrelated area. For example, technology which originated from the US space program has been further developed and applied in many other areas of life. And one certainly cannot depend on government bureaucracies to make accurate as-

143

sessments about these matters.

Another problem is that, where one government might decide to ban the use of a new technology, another country may well go ahead with its introduction. In an increasingly competitive global economy, the first country may severely disadvantage itself by such inaction.

New technology is essential for a country's economic development. The best approach is to positively encourage the development of new technologies and to focus on their benefits. Any problems that may arise can be dealt with after implementation. (275 words)

144

Task1.

主体段第一句: According to the (图表名称)

As shown in the (...)

As can be seen from the (...) that

We can see from the (...) that

It is manifest from the (...) that

第2句: 具体来说: To be more exact, ...

More specifically, ...

More precisely, ...

show →
- describe
- illustrate
- demonstrate
- summarise
- indicate
- display

附　录

Writing Task 1　常用表达法天天背

Expressing movement:

verbs	nouns
rose (to)	a rise
increased to	an increase
went up to	growth
climbed to	an upward trend
boomed	a boom (a dramatic rise)
fell (to)	a decrease
declined (to)	a decline
decreased (to)	a fall
dipped (to)	a drop
dropped (to)	a slump (a dramatic fall)
went down (to)	a reduction
reduced (to)	
levelled out (at)	a levelling out
did not change	no change
remained stable (at)	
remained steady (at)	
stayed (at)	
stayed constant (at)	
maintained the same level	
fluctuated (around)	a fluctuation

升

降

平

波动

rocket v. 猛涨，急速增升 145

平飞

稳定在一个水平上

JR peaked (at)   reached a peak (of)

reach the highest point at
reach the lowest point at

☆ stood at (use this phrase to focus on a particular point, before we mention the movement, for example: In the first year, unemployment stood at...)

Describing the movement:

adjectives	adverbs
dramatic	dramatically
sharp	sharply
huge	
enormous	enormousely
steep	steeply
substantial	substantially
considerable	considerably
significant	significantly
marked	markedly
moderate	moderately
slight	slighty
small	
minimal	minimally

※ 底部

reach the bottom at
reach the lowest at.
point

"占" 多少.

make up. 30% of
occupy. the proportion

account for.

"到达 多少 数量

reach.
arrive at
amount to.
stand at

Describing the speed of change:

Adjective	Adverbs
rapid	rapidly
quick	quickly
swift	swiftly
sudden	suddenly
steady	steadily
gradual	gradually
slow	slowly

预测的
expect
ref predict.

分别. respectively.

146

曲线图常用表达

常见曲线图变化趋势	动词表达	用名词作同义替换表达
↗	rose (to)	a rise (in)
	increased (to)	an increase (in)
	went up (to)	a growth (in)
	climbed (to)	an upward trend (in)
	boomed	a boom in (a dramatic rise) in
↘	fell (to)	a decrease (in)
	declined (to)	a decline (in)
	decreased (to)	a fall (in)
	dipped (to) / dropped (to)	a drop (in)
	went down (to) / slumped (to)	a slump in (dramatic fall in)
	reduced (to)	a reduction (in)
→	levelled out (at)	a levelling out (of)
	did not change	
	remained stable (at)	
	remained steady (at)	no change (in)
	stayed constant (at)	
	maintained the same level	
⋀⋁	fluctuated (around)	a fluctuation (in)
	peaked (at)	reached a peak (of)
	plateaued (at)	reached at plateau (at)
	stood at (we use this phrase to focus on a particular point, before we mention the movement, for example: in the first year, unemployment stood at...)	

147

Writing Task **2** 常用表达法天天背

参见本书30篇范文的万能句子部分,确定目标:每天背完一篇范文后的万能句子,这样大家一个月后就可以完成全部范文后的万能句子,这将是一笔宝贵的写作财富!

✽ 表示递进关系的经典表达法

and

High level positions are stressful at times, and can be harmful to your health.

in addition, additionally, furthermore, moreover, also

High level positions are stressful at times; furthermore, they can be harmful to your health

not only...but also

Not only are high level positions stressful at times, but they also can be harmful to your health.

in addition to, along with, as well as

Along with being stressful, high level positions can also be harmful to your health.

✽ 表示因果关系的经典表达法

for (cause), so (effect)

Professionals can sometimes be extremely impatient, for their positions are at times rather stressful.

because, since

Since high level positions are at times rather stressful, professionals can sometimes be extremely impatient.

therefore, as a result, consequently

High level positions are at times rather stressful; therefore, professionals can sometimes be extremely impatient.

because of, due to, as a result of

Due to the stressful nature of high level positions, professionals can sometimes be extremely impatient.

❋ 表示比较关系的经典表达法

and...too

High level positions are stressful, and can be harmful to your health too.

just as

Just as high level positions are stressful, they can be harmful to your health.

similarly, in comparison

High level positions are stressful at times; similarly, they can be harmful to your health.

like, similar to

Similar to other important professions, high level business positions are stressful at times

❋ 表示对比关系的经典表达法

but

High level positions are stressful at times, but the financial rewards make these positions very desirable indeed.

whereas, while

While high level positions are stressful at times, the financial rewards make these positions very desirable indeed.

in contrast, on the other hand

High level positions are stressful at times; on the other hand, the financial rewards make these positions very desirable indeed.

unlike

Unlike the undesirable stress of high level positions, the financial rewards make these positions very desirable indeed.

❋ 表示条件关系的经典表达法

not withstanding. P₃/₃.

if, unless, only if, even if 即使

If you consider the financial rewards of high level positions, the stressful nature of these positions becomes less important.

otherwise

You should remember the financial rewards of high level positions; otherwise, you might find the stressful nature of these positions too demanding.

149

参考文献

1 Sahanaya W, Lindeck J, Stewart R. Preparation and Practice-Reading and Writing Academic Module. Oxford University Press, 2003

2 Bemmel E, Tucker J. IELTS to Success. John Wiley & Sons Australia, Ltd., 1997

3 Garbutt M, O'Sullivan K. IELTS Strategies for Study, 2002

4 McCarter S, Ash J. IELTS Testbuilder, 2003.

5 Jakeman V, McDowell C. Cambridge Practice Tests for IELTS 1. Cambridge University Press, 2002

6 Jakeman V, McDowell C. IELTS Practice Tests-Plus. Longman, 2002

7 O'Connell S. Focus On IELTS. Longman, 2002